"Biology is an iterative expression of beauty. In order to reach its highest expression, it requires enormous friction. Humanity has spent the last few thousand years as a species at war. We now find ourselves on the brink of extinction as our war waged not just against one another but against the biology beneath our feet from which we are made. If we are to go into right relationship with our nature to go on to thrive, we are going to have to transform within the wound of war. We are going to have to learn to transmute the darkness into light through the power of the human heart and grounded in the silence of the womb of our new humanity. Eva Dalak takes us through her decades of work in war-torn communities around the world to reveal a process of human transformation. Come into stillness here and begin the process within yourself."

- *Zach Bush, MD*

"*Dancing in the Dark* is a profound meditation on how deep loss can be a doorway to transformation. Having been privy to Eva's journey from literal blindness to a grounded and inspiring vision for herself and the world, I am moved by her book and the framework she offers readers for navigating uncertainty and making meaning from the unexpected. Her integration of personal healing with the larger work of peace building demonstrates an embodied understanding of how true change begins within. It has been and continues to be an honor to take part in Eva's work as a member of the Peace Activation community, witnessing firsthand how her methodology—as outlined in this book—provides a practical roadmap for building peace from the inside out. *Dancing in the Dark* is so much more than a story of recovery; it is a light for anyone seeking a path toward soul-centered living, deeply relevant in our fractured world."

- *Toby Israel, founder of Mujeres Fuertes Autodefensa and Choose Empowerment*

"Rich in insight and truth, *Dancing in the Dark* takes the reader on a journey of self-inquiry, empowering each of us to remember that wholeness exists beyond borders and divisions."

- Noa Baum, author of A Land Twice Promised: An Israeli Woman's Quest for Peace

"This is not a self-indulgent recount of one woman's troubles. Instead, it is an honest, intelligent, and bravely depicted account of the struggle we all have with conflict. Conflict of the heart, conflict of the soul, and conflict in our fragmented world. Eva offers a clear heart-centered path to help navigate such times. Although her story is a personal experience, it illuminates the twists and turns we all encounter in our own lives. *Dancing in the Dark* reminds us all to look within for the answers to our own conflicts and gives a reminder that healing grows from love ... Love is the answer."

- Vav Simon, DC AMC FRCC

"*Dancing in the Dark* fills my heart with gratitude and my spirit with inspiration. Eva's leadership is a living reminder that true leaders guide us not only in the light but even more so in the dark."

- Dalit Eliahu Borantin, spiritual psychologist, facilitator and entrepreneur in the field of consciousness

"This book is a courageous journey through grief, identity, loss, and renewal. It calls on the reader to live more authentically and encourages us to find strength in vulnerability and interdependence. The themes of surrendering to illusions of control and achievement are very relatable—a rare gift for anyone seeking meaning in the midst of suffering."

- Catherine Murupaenga-Ikenn, Indigenous activist, educator, and consultant

"In *Dancing in the Dark*, Eva Dalak turns personal loss into a universal path of vision and peace. Her story reminds us that what we choose to see defines our reality and that, even amidst conflict, presence is a radical act. This book is a rare gift—both a witness to healing and a guide toward soul purpose."

- *Anna Penenberg, author of* Dancing in the Narrows

DANCING
IN
THE
DARK

DANCING IN THE DARK

*how i found my true
vision for peace*

EVA DALAK

AWAKEN  VILLAGE

——— PRESS ———

This is a work of nonfiction. Any resemblance to persons living or dead should be plainly apparent to them and those who know them, especially if the author has been kind enough to have provided their real names. All events described herein are true from the author's perspective.

The content of this book is for general instruction only. Each person's physical, emotional, and spiritual condition is unique. The instruction in this book is not intended to replace or interrupt the reader's relationship with a counselor, physician, or other mental health professional.

Editing by Grace Adamarie Watson
Cover and interior design by Andrea Gibb

ISBN 978-1-957408-25-5 (paperback)
ISBN 978-1-957408-26-2 (ebook)

Library of Congress Control Number: 2025917357

Published by Awaken Village Press, Sioux Falls, SD
www.awakenvillagepress.com

To my mother and father, my sisters and brothers, my husband and children, my direct family and soul family, to all the friends around the world who have crossed my path, to all of you who have touched my heart and soul.

"*Your vision will become clear only when you look into your heart. Who looks outside, dreams; who looks inside, awakes.*"

~ *Carl Jung*

preface

I feel pure gratitude as I watch the sunset from the balcony of my new home in Caña Blanca overlooking the Pacific Ocean in Costa Rica. The beauty before me is mesmerizing; it's been so long since I've been able to see such a sight.

At the beginning of 2020, I lost ninety percent of my vision. It happened so abruptly, like a high-speed train coming to an unexpected halt.

Before I lost my sight, I was known for a different kind of vision.

For over twenty-five years, I worked as an international consultant, gender expert, facilitator, and trainer—moving through the worlds of development cooperation, peace building, and conflict transformation. My work took me to some of the most complex and fragile regions in Africa, the Middle East, and Southeast Asia. I've walked into war zones, refugee camps, and government ministries, offering guidance on the Women, Peace and Security Agenda; gender main-streaming; and post-conflict recovery. I've served as a senior advisor for the United Nations, the European Union, and the World Bank, and I've collaborated with countless NGOs and academic institutions.

Educated in international law and administration at the Sorbonne and Robert Schuman universities in France, I have contributed to the implementation and analysis of global frameworks such as CEDAW, UNSCR 1325, the Beijing Platform, the SDGs, and MDGs. I have co-authored country gender analyses for Iraq, Libya, Afghanistan, and Yemen and developed training modules for peacekeeping missions and EU staff, always with a focus on transforming systems and shifting narratives.

I am a polyglot; Arabic is my mother tongue, and I speak French, English, Spanish, and Hebrew fluently. But, more than any language, I've come to understand that human connection—the capacity to listen deeply, to hold complexity, to create space in the midst of conflict—is the real foundation of peace work.

I am also a spiritual counselor, having studied at the University of Santa Monica spiritual psychology and delved deep into all theories and practices of personal development and beyond. And yet, no matter how many training sessions I facilitated or reports I wrote or counseling sessions I received and gave, nothing prepared me for the moment when I had to face my own inner rupture.

The loss of my eyesight was not the end of my story, but the beginning of a deeper one. It stripped me of the roles and identities I'd carried for decades and asked me to meet myself again, not as an expert, but as a human being. As a woman learning to see without her eyes and lead from a place far more tender and true than I had ever known.

Since then, after a two-year healing journey, I have regained my vision, although the healing process continues even three years later. The process of losing and regaining my vision has instilled in me a new sense of responsibility for my life. It has deepened my connection to myself, encouraging me to listen closely to my heart and commit to self-care. I've learned to set stronger, healthier boundaries with my family, friends, and work. The experience has allowed a new way of being to emerge within me, one that is more yin, feminine, and being-oriented, as opposed to my very yang, masculine, and action-oriented self of the past.

I believe that, collectively, we are all moving in this direction, each of us adding our own unique colors and words. For me, this includes serving and inspiring others, whether through my work in conflict zones, my coaching, or my community leadership. And, today, that same passion seeks a new expression, shaped by vision loss, deep listening, and a call to embody peace from within.

Writing this book is part of that journey. It is my story, my perspective on the two years I lived without sight. It is my personal account of what this healing journey has entailed, with themes whose roots stretch back to my childhood as a Palestinian in Israel. Perhaps they stretch even further, into our collective histories themselves.

The final pieces of this book made something clear: everything I've lived through has been a precursor to what is now emerging. My experiences of losing and regaining sight, of identity, of clarity, of purpose, have become the foundations of a deeper calling. That calling is *Peace Activation*: a movement born from the belief that personal healing is the doorway to collective transformation. Through Peace Activation, I've begun to create spaces for truth-telling, for inner reconciliation, and for remembering our shared humanity, especially in places torn apart by division and silence.

This journey has shown me that healing is not a private affair. It ripples outward. It reshapes the world. And, right now, the world is aching for this kind of work—for spaces that are trauma-informed, heart-led, and radically honest. We are living through a time of great unraveling and reimagining, where the systems that once defined us are no longer holding. But, underneath the grief and uncertainty, I sense a powerful emergence: a collective yearning for authenticity, healing, and peace rooted in the soul.

In sharing my story, I aim to break the cycle of selective sight. I want to face the entirety of my history, my identity, and my experiences head-on. By doing so,

I hope to inspire others to look beyond their immediate survival strategies and embrace the full spectrum of their lives. Only by seeing clearly can we truly heal and transform our collective narrative.

I invite you to receive this as a story, not a prescription. Some parts may resonate; others may not. I'm not here to offer advice on what healing *should* look like. Rather, I hope to inspire you to lean into your own journey in your own time. This is simply my experience, shared as I have lived and felt it. The meaning it holds will depend on where you are when it meets you.

I am honored to share this story with you. It has been a challenging creation story filled with doubts, fear, and uncertainty. I've had to make a daily commitment to show up in a whole different way than I used to, needing daily reminders that it is not about me, even though it is my story. Each one of us is a gift in this life, and by learning about one another's gifts, we sometimes discover our own.

There is so much more I wish to share. Our stories never truly end. Each day offers a blank page to write something new. I hope that mine inspires you to bring awareness to your own because your story matters. You matter. And, somewhere in the telling, we begin to remember that peace is not something we wait for. It is something we become.

"Grief is like the ocean;
it comes in waves,
ebbing and flowing.
Sometimes the water is
calm, and sometimes it is
overwhelming. All we can
do is learn to swim."

~ Vicki Harrison

chapter one

DANCING WITH GRIEF

I have always loved dancing. As a girl and young adult, performing was everything to me, an intoxicating blend of freedom and expression that I feared would vanish with adulthood's demands for seriousness. My passion for justice and women's rights seemed destined to overshadow my love for dance, relegating it to childhood memory. But that changed in 2012 at the Burning Man festival. The air was thick with the desert's heat, and the rhythmic beats of electronic music pulsed through the makeshift campgrounds. The scent of dried sand and sweat mixed with the distant whiffs of incense and burning wood, creating an atmosphere of raw, unfiltered human energy.

The dance floor was a kaleidoscope of bodies, all moving in chaotic synchrony, lost in their own rhythms.

I was covered in a thin layer of dust, my skin glistening with sweat under the flashing lights. As I twirled and swayed, feeling the music deep in my bones, my eyes closed. Then, something compelled me to open my eyes, and I noticed him. Fabrice.

Fabrice was a vision amidst the revelry, his presence commanding yet serene. His eyes met mine, and for a moment, the world outside the dance floor ceased to exist. He moved with a grace and confidence that drew me in, and soon, we were dancing together, our movements an unspoken conversation.

Meeting Fabrice ignited a shift in me. My career, which had been focused on law and advocacy, seemed to pause, allowing another part of me to emerge. This was a paradox I hadn't anticipated, finding deeper meaning and identity through dance and connection.

Our journey as a couple took us to various locations: Burning Man, the Ivory Coast, California, New York, and, finally, Costa Rica. We built a beautiful nest in the jungle, gave birth to two beautiful boys unassisted—more on this later—and eventually moved from the Caribbean coast to the South Pacific coast.

Life in Costa Rica had been a blend of adventure and serenity. However, amidst the tropical paradise, an unexpected chapter began to unfold. It started subtly, almost imperceptibly, but it would eventually lead me into one of the darkest periods of my life.

The morning of February 9, 2018, started like no other. We were staying at the Inanitah community in Nicaragua for a month, and I woke up feeling the familiar urge to reach for my phone and check messages, but something inside me hesitated. Instead, I decided to join Gaia's movement class. I moved slowly at first, letting my body wake up with gentle stretches and soft steps. The rhythm of the music at the yoga shala nearby gradually filled me, and soon I was dancing with abandon, feeling a rare sense of freedom and joy. It was a moment of pure connection to myself, unburdened by the digital noise that usually greeted me each day. By the time I checked my phone at 9:00 a.m. instead of my usual 6:00 a.m., it was already too late.

When I heard the news that my father had died, my whole body trembled, overcome by the enormity of my loss. I heard my mom's voice on the message she had left me. "Your dad gave you his life," she said. In Arabic, this is a common way of saying someone has passed; it carries both finality and love.

But when I heard those words in my mother's voice, they landed differently. It wasn't just an announcement of his death; it was a transmission. A reminder that his life had been poured into mine. That his love, his sacrifices, his quiet strength—all of it now lived through me. He did give me his life. He gave me *my* life. I have yet to realize the full extent of what he gave me.

I hadn't seen my dad for six months when my mother's message came. I didn't have the chance to give him a proper hug, say a proper goodbye or "I love you,

Dad." My dad, my baba, had already passed away, transitioned, left his body. None of these words expresses the heartbreak and devastation I felt when I heard the news. I simply had never imagined it happening, nor how broken it would make me feel. It was as if someone hit me in the back with an ax.

The grief came in waves. I cried my heart out. Again and again and again. I cried as I felt his love and tenderness enveloping me, remembering his teachings, his wisdom, and his compassion. My deepest regret was not being there when my father died. Stranded on an island in Nicaragua, it took me over two days to return home to my family in Israel.

Each hour was filled with an increasing sense of despair and regret. I hadn't fully grasped the strength of the powerful foundation my parents had given me, of unconditional love, respect, and service, until I returned to Israel and encountered the fractured lives of others around me. It was then that I understood just how deeply I had been held.

Furthermore, I hadn't realized how much my dad had my back. He was my back. My support. He was my pillar, even when I was nowhere near him. Even though I left my hometown at the age of nineteen and I had been living away from home for twenty-four years, I realized through the process of losing my dad that he never ceased to lift me—completely, unconditionally, subconsciously.

He had always been a man of service—never with

fanfare, but with an unwavering presence. I remember him mediating between neighbors on the verge of divorce, sitting with them for hours until their anger softened into silence. I remember the times he signed as a guarantor for friends or relatives who couldn't afford a mortgage, trusting in people when banks wouldn't. And I remember the harder moments—the nights of shouting between him and my mother, when emotions would erupt and I would try to step in. He would look at me gently but firmly and say, "This is not yours to hold. You don't yet understand what lies in between."

Even in conflict, he carried complexity. He wasn't perfect, but he held contradictions with dignity. That's what stayed with me. He taught me that peace isn't the absence of tension; it's the willingness to stay in the room when things get hard. To show up for others even when your own heart is heavy. That is the life he gave me.

It's revealing to witness how we all hold and express our grief differently. For many of us, there is great discomfort in sitting still for long periods, and we need to get up, change activities, and sit back down. This different dimension of dancing is how I often found myself processing the big emotions. My mother grieved differently. She locked her emotions into the television, into endless Turkish telenovelas and verses from the Quran. That became her ritual, her rhythm of loss.

I didn't know how to grieve at home in Israel. There was space for tears, but not for true emotional expression. In our home, there was no space to speak of feelings. No language for sorrow or fear. That silence, I now realize, shaped so much of who I became. It taught me to internalize pain, to equate strength with independence, to survive by doing rather than feeling. It's only now, looking back, that I can trace the thread from those unspoken griefs to the deep longing I carried for freedom and the cost that came with it.

We cried, yes—but we didn't talk about what we were feeling. And for me, words are everything. They're how I process, how I release. I carried a quiet grief over not being able to mourn my father in words, believing that when I could name something, I could begin to let it go. But in my father's death, the words stayed stuck. I judged myself for what had happened and what wasn't being said.

Why is it that when we most need to talk, we close down, and when we most need to connect and grieve together, we move apart? Is it because we are afraid to feel with a capital F? Is it because the depth of the sorrow, that insatiable longing to be with a loved one, is beyond what we think we can handle? It is as if grief opens up a Pandora's box we're afraid we'll never be able to close, like there will never be an end to the tears.

The loss leaves a hole that we want to ignore, a wound that we don't want to touch. We want to cover it with a band-aid instead of allowing it to air out and scab over naturally. We stop thinking about the person or thing we have lost because the memories reopen the wound, and exposure comes with the risk of accidentally bumping against it. So, we cover it up with food, distraction, or ignorance. We stop ourselves from sharing the stories. Because if we share the stories, then the person's absence is magnified. Celebrating their life means acknowledging its end.

For a long time, I couldn't find solid ground. The structure of my identity had been shattered, dissolving everything I had built around certainty, purpose, and control. I lost interest in the work that had once driven me. I felt hollow and directionless, drowning in a deep depression I didn't know how to name. Everything I had built, my professional identity, my strength, even my sense of clarity, began to fall away.

And yet, in that darkness, something else was also happening. The rawness of the loss was causing something unexpected to emerge. I couldn't understand it, and I certainly couldn't explain it at the time, but I began to feel my father again, not just as memory or legacy but as presence. In moments of stillness, his spirit would brush against mine. I would remember something he used to say or feel his words echo inside my chest as if he were still speaking them. Sometimes I could sense his warmth in my heart as though he was right there beside me, quietly guiding me from the inside.

It was comforting and confusing. I didn't have the language to describe what was happening. I only knew I wasn't alone, even as I was unraveling. My dad's death had shattered my reality as an independent woman, and I realized how much he had been holding my structure together, supporting me in the ether and teaching me wisdom without clearly articulating it. The more I felt his presence again, the more I realized how much of him lived in me, and that both softened and deepened the grief.

I realized later that the morning I got the news of his death, I was actually with my father in spirit as he passed to the other realm. I felt a sense of his presence as I was called to dance and avoided the pull of my phone. He was there, guiding me to cherish the simple, present moments. In that dance, I realized my father had given me not only his life but also his last dance, a gift of presence and freedom that I will carry with me always. Through his absence, I would learn to connect more deeply with myself and those around me, finding new ways to express love and gratitude for the life he had given me.

My father's death didn't just break my heart; it broke the frame through which I had understood life, purpose, and even myself. This marked the beginning of my descent into darkness—a slow, quiet unraveling of everything I thought I knew. It was as if his passing opened a doorway I wasn't ready to walk through, into grief, into questioning, into the unknown.

I was walking through the darkest season of my life, and yet there was this quiet light, a presence I could feel but not hold. It brought me to my knees, not just in sorrow but in awe. That was the paradox: The more I surrendered to the pain, the more connected I became to something beyond me. And that connection—unseen, wordless, alive—would eventually guide me toward a new kind of vision.

Back in Costa Rica, it was hard for me to comprehend that my father was gone, as he was so present. I heard him talking to me, his sentences and even some of our disagreements. But my life was overflowing with busyness, a constant juggling act of identities and responsibilities. I was a mother, a wife, a consultant, a coach. I was facilitating in conflict zones one month and tending to our jungle farm the next. I held space for others' healing while trying to make sense of my own. There was a multiplicity of being—of roles, of geographies, of emotional landscapes—that kept me moving, held together by momentum more than presence. And, somewhere within all that motion, I began to lose sight of myself—quietly, gradually, until my body began to speak what I could not name.

In July, a few months after my dad's death, a hole in my retina was identified. This rupture in my vision became the first signal that something deeper was shifting, both physically and emotionally, and it seemed to mirror the invisible hole left by his absence. It marked the beginning of a journey through loss, a journey of seeing differently, of grieving what was no longer visible, and of learning to navigate the world with a heart and body forever changed.

This initial indication that there was a problem with my eyesight was a symbolic moment for the start of a journey: the journey of loss. But I found it easier to involve myself in activities that took my mind off my sadness rather than face the diagnosis, even though I knew that it would only make the route to healing more difficult. It was too hard for me to sit with all of the sadness and grief over both forms of loss at once. So, I brushed it off and tried to get through each day.

I didn't take my doctor's warnings seriously when my vision was first inspected. There was always something more urgent—another meeting, another trip, another crisis to tend to. After all, I was holding so much, between children, work, clients, communities, and stories of war and healing. Getting a full eye exam, with scans and detailed imaging to understand the growing black spot in my retina, had felt like something I could just postpone. I kept telling myself it was just stress, fatigue, the price of doing too much. But the symptoms didn't go away—they intensified. My body had been whispering, but I wasn't listening. And that hole kept growing, quietly becoming the shadow that would change everything.

On an intellectual level, I know that whenever we lose something or somebody we love, it is important to take time out for ourselves and truly feel the weight of what we are experiencing. But I wasn't operating on an intellectual level. I wasn't thinking about what I was experiencing—I was inside of it.

Emotionally, I was being undone. The waves came without warning, sometimes soft and sometimes relentless. Grief surfaced in unexpected places, brushing up against memories, regrets, and a longing that had no words. I was meeting parts of myself I didn't even know were still grieving.

Physically, it was as though my body remembered everything I had tried to forget. A dull ache in my chest. Sleepless nights. A heaviness in my limbs. Even my eyesight began to falter, as if my body was insisting that I pause and look inward. That I see not just what was lost but what was trying to emerge.

Spiritually, too, something had cracked open. My father's death left a silence I couldn't fill. But, within that silence, I began to sense another kind of presence—subtle, spacious, and deeply real. It wasn't about understanding grief anymore. It was about surrendering to it. Letting it teach me. Letting it reshape me from the inside out.

Although it may seem that doing so will push us into a deeper state of sadness, truly permitting ourselves to be with whatever arises creates space for us to begin healing. Grieving is a natural process, allowing us to sort through the range of emotions that are present in our everyday existence. This has been a frequent lesson for me throughout the years.

Reflecting on the dynamic nature of life and death, the jungle offers a powerful parallel. It is representative of what Mother Nature looks like when she is amplified in a fuller expression than most humans get to experience. In its constant state of change, the jungle mirrors the rhythm of life itself, teaching us about the beauty and inevitability of transformation.

I remember one time when my son, three years old at the time, looked at me as I was grieving. I could see him trembling, with tears in his eyes, as he asked what was wrong. I told him it was that my dad was gone. He caressed me and then went on with his day, as if this explanation was enough of a reason, and now he could go about looking for a game to play.

I didn't expect that. Maybe my youngest son, having been born and raised in the jungle, has a natural view of birth and death, having been enmeshed in it all his life. Perhaps it was as natural to see me grieving as it was when he had seen dead spiders or fallen trees. He already knew that sadness because living in Costa Rica provided so many opportunities to see life spring out of death almost immediately.

Change happens in every moment of our lives. Since nothing but change is constant, it often feels as if, whenever things shift, we are losing something. We experience both gains and losses. This understanding helped me more readily accept and process whatever happens.

Grief often compels us to hide, to curl inward, to

protect ourselves from more pain. It is a heavy experience. How could it be light? But I've learned that sharing grief can lighten its weight. When we allow someone else to hold part of it with us, we begin to breathe again.

At first, I hesitated. I worried I was being too much, that others were already carrying enough. But then I remembered: If the roles were reversed, I would never want my loved ones to carry their sorrow alone. Their protests about "burdening me" would seem pointless. To truly carry my grief, I would have to let go of everything else I had been holding onto: titles, roles, beliefs, even, at times, hope. This was not a graceful surrender; it was a freefall. And it was only by falling that I would begin to understand what was asking to be born.

That was one of grief's quietest lessons for me. I began to open up to a few friends—Meg, Nes, and Rozanne—and in doing so, I was met not with judgment or discomfort, but with presence. Each of them had experienced her own profound loss: Meg had lost her daughter; Nes, her mother; Rozanne, her grandfather. Because they had walked through their own grief, they could sit with mine without trying to fix it. They didn't rush me or offer platitudes. They just listened, and, in that sacred listening, something in me began to settle. I could finally speak the words I had been carrying. As I did, I began to let them go.

Sharing grief and embracing vulnerability serve as powerful antidotes to hiding, transforming our pain into a pathway for deeper connection and healing. When we hide our grief, we isolate ourselves, intensifying the weight of our sorrow. However, by sharing our grief, we allow others to help carry our burdens, fostering a sense of solidarity and understanding. This openness creates a bridge between isolation and connection, allowing us to process our emotions more effectively.

I've learned, often the hard way, that unless we listen to where we truly are in the moment, our emotions don't disappear. They only grow louder and heavier, finding other ways to express themselves in our body, spirit, and relationships. For a long time, I avoided grief. I didn't know how to sit with it, name it, or honor it. But once I began to acknowledge what I was feeling, even when it was messy or painful, I found a kind of relief. A softening. The sorrow didn't vanish, but it stopped haunting me.

Once I allowed myself to feel the fullness of my loss, to cry, tremble, or speak, I also opened the door to healing. Through this, I came to understand that grief doesn't have to trap us in fear or sadness. Slowly, I saw that it, like joy, is a visitor. It passes through. It shapes us. But it doesn't have to define us. This realization didn't come from reading or knowing; it came from surviving, from being broken open and letting life touch me again.

Facing loss head-on is a journey. Even the mundane dance of avoidance is still a dance, but if we can be conscious of what we are avoiding feeling, even that will take us deeper into the next dimension of dancing with the dark. It is a layer-by-layer process that eventually gives us the resilience and courage to be with stillness a little more each time.

When my eyes closed to the world, my soul opened to its memory. I did not fall into darkness—I answered its call. There, I remembered the grief I carried was never mine alone. What breaks us open is sometimes what births us whole.

*"The wound is the place
where the Light enters you."*

~ Rumi

chapter two

BETWEEN WORLDS

When I answered the call of darkness, I didn't just meet my own sorrow; I stepped into a much older grief. One carried by generations before me. To understand my own unraveling, I had to trace the origins of the silence I was born into. And it all started with the things I was taught not to see. It wasn't clearly articulated in that way, but it was the overall sense I got from the variety of experiences I had growing up, and that I can see and reflect on now retrospectively. I didn't see, or better yet didn't want to see, how messed up the situation was. Be it at home or at school, no one spoke of the *Nakba*, Palestine, or Palestinian identity.

Borders do not only exist on maps. They exist in our bodies, our identities, our psyches. They are drawn not just in land but in language, in belonging, in the silent spaces between who we are and who we are allowed to be.

I was born into an identity shaped by political structures long before I took my first breath. Before I could speak or form thoughts of my own, the world had already defined me in ways that were both rigid and impossible. I grew up between worlds: Arab yet Israeli, Palestinian yet stateless, part of the system yet outside of it. My very existence was a contradiction, a puzzle that did not quite fit into the neat boxes the world prefers.

But these contradictions were not just personal struggles. They were the byproduct of borders, laws, and a historical reality designed to fragment people like me. I was not simply experiencing confusion; I was inheriting a conflict, living inside a structure that had been built long before I was born. And this structure did not want me to belong fully anywhere—it wanted me to remain divided, uncertain, neither here nor there.

I spent much of my life navigating these invisible borders. In school, in conversations, in airports where my name and my passport told two different stories, I learned that identity was not just something you feel—it is something that is policed, questioned, and sometimes even denied. And yet, despite these barriers, something within me refused to be fragmented. There was a deeper truth beneath the imposed divisions, a knowing that my wholeness existed beyond the borders drawn around me.

My grandparents' generation identified as Palestinians without question. There was no hesitation, no split between citizenship and identity, no need to navigate between worlds. Then, in 1948, everything changed. Some were forced into exile, turned into refugees overnight. Others, like my family, remained in what had suddenly become Israel. They were given Israeli citizenship but treated as second-class citizens, expected to assimilate while never being fully accepted.

The *Nakba*, Arabic for "catastrophe," refers to the mass displacement and dispossession of Palestinians during the 1948 Arab-Israeli war, when more than 750,000 Palestinians were expelled or fled from their homes as the State of Israel was established. Over 400 villages were destroyed or depopulated, and generations have since lived in exile or as second-class citizens in their own homeland. The Nakba is not only a historical event; it is an ongoing experience of loss, fragmentation, and struggle for recognition and return.

This created a generational wound, one that ran deeper than any physical border. Some clung fiercely to an identity that was being erased, teaching their children stories of villages that no longer existed on official maps. Others assimilated out of survival, learning Hebrew, adopting the language and customs of the state that now governed their lives, trying to carve out space in a system that had not been built for them.

And then there were those like me, born into the in-between. I spent years trying to reconcile a past that had been rewritten, a history that had been buried. I wanted to understand the land beneath my feet, but every time I searched, I found conflicting versions of the truth.

What happens to people when their identity is politically weaponized? When being Palestinian is seen as a threat? When being Arab in Israel comes with conditions—conditional rights, conditional acceptance, conditional belonging?

When identity is shaped by colonial structures, it becomes more than just a personal experience—it becomes a battlefield. And I, like so many others, have spent my life walking that battlefield, trying to reclaim something that was taken before I even knew it was mine.

I grew up in a conservative Muslim family, raised on the values of care, compassion, and tolerance. Teachings around the generosity of the heart were woven into daily life. And yet, within that loving foundation, my parents and I often disagreed—over my haircut, my clothes, my habit of reading books while walking or late into the night, and even my desire to go to the beach alone. To them, these were acts of defiance; to me, they were expressions of independence. At the time, I saw this as control. Now, as a parent myself, I recognize the love and fear behind their concerns. Still, they never tried to suppress who I was becoming.

My father, may he rest in peace, often said, "Eva, let's agree to disagree." And so we did. At home, around the dinner table, that same unspoken border remained. We'd sit together, plates full, the smell of rice and spices mingling with the hum of the news in the background—Hebrew news, always. We talked about school, about family, about food, about anything that wasn't too charged. No one mentioned the Nakba. No one said the word "occupation." In our house, love came with silence. My parents believed in harmony, and, in that belief, certain things were never said out loud. But their silence spoke volumes.

It wasn't about avoiding hard conversations. It was about protecting peace and keeping connection alive rather than focusing on being right. In their own way, my family chose harmony over conflict, allowing us to share a deep love despite the differences in our opinions. The quiet grace of my parents' unconditional love and acceptance shaped me more than they'll ever know.

Their way of choosing compassion over control taught me that peace begins in the smallest places: in how we listen, how we show up, how we love. It is what has enabled me to become who I am. It created a space inside of me to accept others, to be tolerant in the face of paradox and seek harmony despite disagreement and differences, accepting people and situations as they are. It's this foundation that eventually became the compass for my work in the world. In every conflict zone I have entered, every circle I have facilitated, and every woman's story I have listened to, I have carried the quiet strength of my parents' values. Even as I lost my vision, I never lost that inner compass. It became my anchor as I stepped into the work of healing myself and others.

But it also taught me, quietly and implicitly, that some things were not meant to be seen or spoken of—like Palestine, the Nakba, or the emotional weight carried silently through generations. So we learned to love and to live with the gaps between what we felt and what we could say. In the name of peace, we allowed silence to hold what couldn't be expressed in words, truths too complex, too painful, or too risky to name aloud. And, in that silence, something was preserved, even if it was never fully seen.

Fast-forward to my time at a French Jesuit school, where what I was taught had no context for or immediate relevance to the conflict I was directly living within. We studied French culture, history, geography, and politics—nothing about how the state of Israel came to be or how Palestine had disappeared from the map. The generation after the Nakba was too traumatized to engage, and if they did engage in politics, they would find themselves either in prison or without a job.

At home, we heard the news from the Israeli perspective, and I was reading books in Hebrew, again from the Israeli perspective. I had no contact or context for any of my own culture, religion, or language. And at school, like at home, speaking about politics was forbidden. We had a few hours of Arabic each week, taught by a man from a nearby Arab village, Ar'ara. He often seemed frustrated by our disinterest, mine included. I didn't like him, and we clashed often enough that I eventually dropped his class.

Looking back, I realize that some of the tension I felt came from the judgments I carried. As a girl from the city, I looked down on him, not because of who he was, but because of the lenses I had inherited. He wasn't "cool." He wasn't polished. And, somewhere deep inside, I had absorbed the Jewish-Israeli disdain toward Arab villagers—especially *falahin*, the rural working class. I, too, had internalized the hierarchy. I even used to call myself an "Israeli Arab," unconsciously distancing myself from the word *Palestinian*. At the time, I didn't realize what I was erasing, what had already been erased for me.

That's what I was taught at the Arab-Jewish community center I attended. There was no mention of any connection to Palestinians in the occupied territories or even in the diaspora. You see, I've always lived between worlds. Arab but Israeli. Palestinian but stateless. Raised in Jaffa, I moved fluidly between Hebrew, Arabic, and French, between hummus and schnitzel, between silences and the truths they concealed. I had to go through an identity crisis to find belonging and connection.

When I was fifteen I had the opportunity to travel to Eastbourne, UK, with a group from the

Arab-Jewish community center in Jaffa. I went there with two other Israeli Jewish girls from the center to take part in a theater workshop called "Peace Child," a play about children seeking peace in conflict zones. It was my first time traveling outside of Israel. It was also my first encounter with Israeli airport security, and the experience turned out to be painful.

We arrived with our parents, full of excitement at Ben Gurion Airport, where that in-between is no metaphor; it's palpable. I handed over my passport and watched the security officer's eyes scan my name. "Dalak." A pause. A flicker of suspicion.

Questions followed. Where was I born? Where was I going? Why? I was pulled aside for "additional screening," my bags opened, my belongings sifted through, my body subtly but firmly reminded: you don't quite belong. The fathers of the two Jewish girls, who held high ranks in the army, intervened in the security agents' investigation. This stroke of "luck" allowed me to travel.

We were in the UK for a month, staying with host families as we prepared to perform in Eastbourne. But during the improvisation sessions, I found myself holding back. We were a diverse group—people from conflict zones and European countries—and each of us was asked to express how we felt and what the point of conflict was in our lives. I was around Arabs who were proud of their identity. It was a new experience for me. This was unlike my experience in Israel, where many were under occupation, in prison for speaking up, or living in fear of doing so.

When the spotlight was on me, I felt hesitant and concealed my thoughts, unsure of what to share. I struggled to find inspiration, but finally, my turn came, and I felt as though I had no choice. The girl before me, who was from Switzerland, had shared that she felt ashamed to live in a peaceful country while many of her friends lived in conflict. Initially, I felt jealous and thought she was being foolish. She was lucky and didn't seem to appreciate it. It was then that I realized what I needed to say.

I named my identities. I am a girl, I am Arab, I am Muslim, and I am Israeli. Each of these identities was its own conflict. I did not have a reference for myself as Palestinian, even in my discourse.

When I left home at the age of nineteen, four years later, that was when I really "discovered" my "Palestinianhood." I received a scholarship from the French government to study law in Strasbourg. That was the beginning of my journey abroad, away from home, and the start of my journey into becoming a peaceworker—though, at the time, I didn't call it that.

My identity as a Palestinian came to the forefront when the Jewish community invited me to celebrate Shabbat with them after learning I came from Israel. I accepted with delight. I was longing for belonging, and that community was the closest I knew to home. I knew the traditions and I understood the language.

But when they discovered in our discussions that I was Muslim and not Jewish, they withdrew the invitation. For me, it was the first time that I had such a distinction that Israel is associated only with Jewish people. How could it be, I thought to myself, that people outside of Israel didn't know what was going on inside of Israel? The diversity of the ethnic groups living together—the Muslims, the Jews, the Christians, the Circassians, the Armenians, and others?

Three years later, while working on my master's thesis about human rights in Palestine, I came face-to-face with a harsh reality that shook me to the core. The more I researched, the more I realized that Israel was not just a "democracy in the Middle East," as I had been taught; it was also an occupying power, systematically violating the rights of Palestinians living under its control. I couldn't sleep at night. I had nightmares. I was consumed by confusion, caught between two identities that no longer made sense together.

My research confronted me with the narratives I had absorbed all my life, stories from Jewish literature and education that described the land of Palestine as empty, desolate, filled with malaria, and uplifted only through Zionist settlement. I had believed, or at least never questioned, that version of history. But suddenly, I discovered a rich, vibrant Palestinian and Arab culture that had existed long before 1948, one that had been erased not only from public discourse but from my own consciousness.

I felt betrayed. My family, my school, my community, none had given me the context for where we were living or what had happened. The Nakba, the occupation, even the word *Palestinian*, none of it had been part of the story I was raised with. I now understand this silence as a trauma response, a coping mechanism formed for the sake of surviving within a system that was designed to erase and divide. I felt ashamed of my own ignorance, of having lived in a French-speaking bubble at a Jesuit school in Jaffa, oblivious to the tragedy unfolding just outside its gates.

Once I completed my master's degree, I returned home with the illusion that I could now work as a lawyer in *my* country. At the time, I still considered Israel my country. But that illusion shattered quickly. Within a month, I came face to face with the deep-rooted discrimination embedded in every layer of the system.

I remember one interview at a well-known law firm in Haifa. The conversation started off politely enough, until the inevitable question came: "Where did you serve in the army?" I replied honestly, "I didn't." The air shifted immediately. The interviewer glanced down, mumbled something about qualifications, and wrapped it up quickly. I never heard back. It was clear: my degree, my skills, my passion didn't matter as much as my absence from the military. That's when it hit me that not serving wasn't just a checkbox I'd missed. It marked me that silently but powerfully, as someone who didn't belong.

I finally managed to find an internship at UNESCO in Paris, and later on, I joined a team at an International NGO based in Brussels. That was my final initiation. I was responsible for the Middle East program, and it was then that I learned the various discourses and narratives about the conflict. What struck me most at the time was how discussing Palestinian suffering always required an immediate reference to Jewish loss. This left little room for the legitimate expression of Palestinian pain and trauma.

And so, for most of my life, I didn't claim my identity as a Palestinian. I integrated it into the variety of cultures and identities in each place I visited, lived, or worked. Being Palestinian was an add-on, not the focus. I didn't yet have the language to describe it, but I could feel it: I was on the inside, yet always on the margins.

"I saw more clearly with my
eyes closed than I had ever
seen with them open."

~ Inspired by Lakota
vision quest teachings

chapter three

A QUEST FOR VISION

I lost my vision progressively over four years, so slowly that I didn't notice. First, it just grew blurry and foggy, like looking through a smudged lens. Then, I could no longer distinguish the letters on a page. I could see outlines, but not details. Faces became shadows. Reading became a strain, then a struggle, and eventually something I had to give up.

It didn't happen overnight, but it took me by surprise when, one day, I tried to read a terms of reference for a new contract on my computer and realized I couldn't. It was like the world was slowly dimming around me, and I was powerless to stop it.

It was December 2019, and I finally had to acknowledge that I couldn't see. In shock, I decided to book an appointment with an ophthalmologist in San Jose, a five-hour drive from where I lived on the Caribbean coast of Costa Rica. One month later, after an hour and a half of various exams on different machines, the doctor concluded that I was losing my vision due to burned retinas, a condition linked to sun gazing and exacerbated by the eclipses.

Indeed, I had been practicing sun gazing, an early morning ritual where I would connect with the energy of the sun, especially in those quiet moments just after sunrise. It was never about technique or discipline; it was about presence. For me, the sun represents unconditional love, a force that shines on all beings without judgment or distinction, regardless of who we are or where we stand. In those moments of direct connection, I felt a deep alignment with the divine, the Earth, and the spark of power within myself. It was my way of remembering that I, too, am made of light. That I belong.

The doctor warned me that, unless we operated immediately, I would completely lose my vision. He added that, even if I underwent the operation, I wouldn't necessarily regain my full vision but that, at least, I wouldn't lose any more.

I thought he was dramatic, as if he were trying to manipulate me into agreeing to surgery. Later, I consulted a third doctor at an eye institute, who explained that my eyesight loss was a normal and natural function of aging, just accelerated in my case, similar to a woman in her seventies. Thinking I knew better than the medical advice I was receiving, I decided to seek alternative solutions, hoping to uncover the emotions behind my vision loss and work it out myself, at least until I could return home to Israel to visit my family and maybe get another checkup there. It felt like the safer option.

Back in my house in the jungle, I spent the next three months trying out various local alternative medicines. I put honey, urine, and castor oil in my eyes. I experimented with plant medicine and energy healing, psychoanalysis, spiritual counseling, biofeedback, bioresonance, and soul regression. All just to understand why this was happening. What was this experience here to teach me?

As I sought to heal my eyesight, I was finally able to access my true feelings of deep loss and desolation. Deep in multiple layers of grief now, I stopped eating. Food didn't taste like anything because there was no emotion there. I was able to stop feeding myself and just let it be. I allowed myself to stop tending to everyone else and simply *be*.

I felt nurtured by Mother Nature in other forms. I let the river hold me and bathed in the warmth of the sun. These nature elements—water, earth, light—fed me in a way no meal ever could. I drank water and let myself *feel*, feel the grief, the exhaustion, the hunger that wasn't about food. I began to see how, in my family, love had been expressed through food—food as care, as control, as the only way we knew how to come together. But here, in the arms of nature, I remembered a different kind of nourishment. One that asked nothing of me and gave everything.

My existence now boiled down to basic survival, self-focused actions, and minimal but meaningful interactions with the outside world. This personal tragedy coincided with the COVID-19 pandemic, a period of global turmoil and uncertainty. People around the world were grappling with unprecedented challenges, isolation, and fear. It felt as though the entire planet was experiencing a collective dark night of the soul.

During the pandemic, while the world turned inward with limited interactions outside of online connections, I didn't even have the comfort of virtual engagement. I spent most of my time in the jungle with my family and a few friends who remained nearby. Each of us, in our own way, tried to make sense of this new reality of separation and confinement. Just as we all needed safe spaces to talk, connect, and embrace the darkness, I found solace in the love and support around me. These connections helped me reclaim a sense of purpose and navigate through my own journey in darkness.

For many months, I struggled to make sense of this new loss and the profound changes in my life. I was persistent in my quest to find meaning in an experience that seemed senseless. It left me grappling with endless questions: Why me? Why now? What did I do wrong? How can I fix it? How can I fix myself? These personal questions echoed the global inquiries we all faced during the pandemic. The world was in turmoil, and our shared suffering underscored our vulnerability and interconnectedness, highlighting the impact of this collective experience.

Without the ability to follow the news, scroll on social media, or participate in any debates, my struggle was internal and profoundly deep. Unable to see what was going on, I dealt with current events on a deeply personal and physical level. I longed for understanding and decided to embark on a journey to confront the things in life I didn't want to see and uncover what was hidden behind my loss of eyesight.

I wasn't seeking a single diagnosis—I was listening, across many modalities, to what my body and spirit were trying to tell me. I worked with different therapists and healers: reiki practitioners who placed their hands gently over my eyes, channeling energy into the places that felt most shut down; psychotherapists who helped me unravel the emotional layers of grief and identity; sound healers whose gongs and crystal bowls vibrated through the parts of me that words couldn't reach. I lay on massage tables for bodywork sessions that unlocked buried memories, received energy healing that stirred long-held sadness, and sat in the presence of intuitive guides who helped me hear the voice beneath the symptoms.

Some healing sessions were quiet and subtle; others left me trembling or in tears. But each one offered another layer of insight into the possible roots of my vision loss. They brought me closer to something essential, a recognition that my vision loss was not just physical. It was an invitation to look inward. To see differently. To begin a conversation with parts of myself I had long ignored.

As a spiritual counselor, I interpreted events differently than most people around me. Was it the wars I had witnessed that now reflected in my eyes? The fires I had endured in past lives? The judgments I held about situations and people? Karma from previous existences? There was so much to investigate.

I was seeking meaning, which, for me, is as essential as the air I breathe. I delved into various disciplines—spiritual psychology, Chinese medicine, acupuncture, Ayurveda, and medical intuition—seeking perspectives into these different disciplines. Was my vision loss a manifestation of anger? A sense of unworthiness? A feeling of loss? A lack of life satisfaction or love? Underneath it all was the constant question: "Why?"

My wake-up call was as cold as ice. I had lost my eyesight. And there was no more work to do, no more family to take care of, no more anyone that mattered. There was nothing else to do but sit and reflect on my life.

At home, life carried on, though I had lost my lust for it. I was still a mother to our two young boys, now six and eight years old, and a wife to Fabrice. But everything felt suspended, like I was floating through the days without direction, desperate for meaning. The life I had once led—full of movement, clarity, control—was no longer available to me. And though I tried to stay strong, part of me was still grieving everything I had lost, unsure of what could ever take its place.

It was a time of deep unraveling, and I couldn't have made it through without Fabrice, who became my guide and my constant companion. He stepped into roles neither of us had anticipated, taking on every task from caring for the boys to managing day-to-day activities, ensuring I felt supported and safe. This profound shift in our relationship required him to adapt quickly and selflessly. He was a pillar for us all as he walked beside me through the darkest parts of the unknown.

I would guide the boys with my voice as we cooked together. I gave them instructions, and they became my eyes, narrating what they saw as they helped me chop or stir. They held my hand when we crossed the street, and Fabrice drove me to the places I needed to go so I wouldn't have to navigate on my own. He took me to healing sessions, held me through emotional waves, and helped me process all of the grief, fear, and confusion. He answered messages, managed logistics, connected with healers and friends, and served as my window to the outside world, since mine had clouded over.

Witnessing his unwavering support, I was in awe of his strength and resilience as he took on these immense responsibilities with grace and determination. He was not just caring for me but also serving as my anchor in a time of deep uncertainty. Each day, he was there, providing a steady presence and helping me navigate my internal struggles.

Fabrice's dedication was not just about helping me through the physical loss of sight; it was about rediscovering our bond and learning to communicate in new, profound ways. Through his eyes, I found my way, and through his strength, I found the courage to face each day. His unwavering support transformed our partnership, revealing depths of love and resilience we had never known before. Their love—his and the boys'—gave me the safety to turn inward. Yet I wasn't able to let go of control and focus on healing. In my despair, I refused to see that I was actually held. I felt abandoned and betrayed by life.

When I experienced the loss of my eyesight, I was shocked and sad, but mostly I felt the urge to withdraw from everything. Once a social butterfly, I transformed into a solitary hermit. I had once found healing through the process of sharing my inner thoughts and grief with others, but now I couldn't find it in me to reach out to those trusted and precious people who cared about me the most. I judged myself for the experience I was having, and I struggled to ask for support. However, the universe spoke to me through many channels, and when I was finally ready to receive its messages, I also received nurturing care from many loving partners in my life journey.

It may seem like remaining withdrawn would protect us from the world, but sharing our vulnerability is the foundation for deep and authentic relationships. Opening ourselves up in this way gets to the core of our being, past all of our defenses and prejudices. When life seems to crack the outer shell of our world, we become both raw and fresh. It is then that we discover who is truly willing to walk with us through challenging times, even if some of those sent to help us may not be who or what we expected. Regardless, we learn to trust in the universe, in others, in our strength and resilience, and in the wisdom of life itself.

Once I opened myself to sharing this grief and asking for help, I committed myself to be of service to my own experience, publicly divulging my healing process with at least a selective group of friends, family, and acquaintances who wanted to be informed. I kept reminding myself that not sharing feelings with others denies them the opportunity to learn, and, once I opened myself up to the idea, the process of sharing felt both natural and helpful. By sharing our hopes and fears, joys and pains with another person, we accept the universe's gifts of wisdom and loving care. We may be the messengers sent by the universe for their benefit. What if this, in fact, is our mission?

For six months, I processed the uncertainty of my life's direction and all the thoughts I was investigating. It was my mom's tears and heartfelt pleas that made me realize how my condition was affecting not just me but also those who loved me. Her words moved me to finally reconsider the surgery the doctor had told me about months prior.

The process of accepting the necessity of the surgery was fraught with resistance and inner turmoil. It wasn't just a simple decision; it was a battle between hope and fear, between belief and mistrust. At the core of my hesitation were several factors that created a sense of paralysis.

Firstly, there was a deep mistrust of Western medicine. My experiences and beliefs as a spiritual counselor had led me to explore alternative healing modalities. I believed that the answers to my health issues could be found in spiritual psychology, Chinese medicine, acupuncture, Ayurveda, and medical intuition. The idea of surgery felt like an abandonment of these beliefs, a surrender to a system I didn't fully trust. This mistrust was reinforced by past experiences where Western medicine had failed to provide holistic care, focusing more on symptoms rather than the root causes of illness.

There was also an added psychological aspect to my resistance. I had always been a caregiver, focusing on others rather than myself. The idea of prioritizing my health felt foreign and selfish. I had already started to resign myself to a life with limited vision, believing that it was my fate and that I had to accept it. This resignation was a form of giving up, a way to avoid the risk and vulnerability that came with hoping for something better.

Adding to this was a deep-seated hope in positive psychology and the power of the mind to heal the body. I believed that, through meditation, affirmations, and inner work, I could restore my vision. Fabrice even suggested an unconventional remedy—putting urine in my eyes. Desperate for a non-surgical solution, I tried it, hoping for a miracle. But as my vision continued to deteriorate, the reality of my situation became undeniable.

Underneath all of this resistance was a profound fear—of the surgery itself, of waking up completely blind, losing the little vision I had left. I was terrified that the procedure might make things worse, leaving me in an even darker place. This paralyzing fear, perhaps more than anything else, was what had prevented me from taking this step.

I confided in two dear friends, Sophie and Meg, who also played a crucial role in convincing me to undergo the surgery. They provided a different perspective, helping me see that accepting the surgery didn't mean abandoning my beliefs but rather integrating them with a practical solution. They offered to help with the logistics, taking over the practical aspects that overwhelmed me.

Looking back, I see how my resistance came from a tangled mix of mistrust, fear, fragile hope, and quiet resignation. It was the steady support of my mother, Fabrice, and close friends that eventually helped me move through those layers and accept the need for surgery. It was a humbling experience—one that taught me healing sometimes asks for both surrender and strength, for faith in medicine and the unwavering presence of those who love us.

On Thursday, August 6, 2020, I arrived at the clinic at 9 a.m. for my surgery. After checking in, I was led away from the comforting presence of Meg's warm energy. I felt cold as the assistant asked me to remove all of my clothes, jewelry, and the crystals I had brought to support me in the process. It all went into a box, and I was handed a plain robe. The assistant then guided me to another room, where the nurses administered a sedative and left me to wait for it to take effect. Then, another assistant brought me to the operating room. What I remember most is the silence, the cold atmosphere, and the bright, clinical lights.

In the midst of the operation, I awoke to hear the surgeon making jokes about my belief in the ability to heal through meditation. I could hardly believe it—there I was, at the mercy of this doctor, and he was making fun of me. I felt vulnerable and helpless, unable to move or speak. My eyes were spread wide open, but I couldn't see. I focused on my breathing and tried to stay calm.

When the surgery was over and both of my eyes were covered, I felt one of the assistants help me into my clothes and escort me to where Meg was waiting. As soon as I felt my friend's arms around me, I released my tension. She held me while I cried, then walked me to the car to drive back to the Airbnb we had rented for the night to be close to the clinic for the following morning's check-up.

That night was a strange experience. I had been living with diminished vision for months, but now I was completely in the dark. With my eyes still covered, I got around by touching the walls, having to ask for help for absolutely everything I needed. Meg prepared dinner for me and helped me eat, identifying where the spoon was, where the plate was, what was on the plate, and how to bring it to my mouth. I felt so powerless, helpless like a baby. I comforted myself by saying that it was only for one night, that tomorrow the cover would be removed and I would be able to see again. I didn't know yet how naive I was, that this was only the beginning of what would be my deepest journey into darkness.

The next day, Meg accompanied me back to the clinic. The doctor removed the gauze and checked my eyes with different machines. It felt so alienating, the bright light, the technology that told him what was going on in my eyes. I couldn't see his face. I couldn't see anything, actually; everything remained a fog. I could sense that I wouldn't be receiving good news, but I was still hoping, waiting for a miracle. I was still expecting to somehow recover my full sight.

The doctor said that it would be a two-week process of closing the holes in the retina and keeping them closed with gauze. I felt I could live with that and was ready to wait patiently for two weeks for the chance to see again. But it actually took two months for the gauze to dissipate.

Words cannot adequately describe my experience of seeing nothing but a clouded veil, like a mountain obscured by mist. Every day became a haunting waiting period of wondering when I would finally wake up and see. My meditation and kundalini practice sustained me, helping me breathe deeply through the process. When the fog finally seemed to clear from my sight, I was surprised to find that, even then, my eyesight still remained blurred.

It hit me then that the surgery hadn't returned my vision to the extent I had hoped it would. I felt lost once again in the darkness around me. I was still almost entirely dependent on my family and friends. I moved from one emotion to another like a chameleon: gratitude for all the support I was receiving, humiliation for needing that support, humility for the experience I was going through, and anger and sadness for that same experience. It was a rollercoaster of rejection, unworthiness, injustice, humiliation, and betrayal. I couldn't find my center.

The surgery, I realized, would only be the beginning. I was confined once again by the boundaries of my own limitations. Throughout this period, the support of my family and friends was invaluable. My friends Meg, Sophie, and Aisha helped with logistics and medical appointments, as well as lifting my spirits with music and dance, helping me navigate the unrelenting darkness.

Unable to see and still wanting to dance, I constantly questioned, "Do I have enough space, Aisha?" Fearful of falling, I hesitated with every step. But my friend was there, playing music like a DJ, filling the room with a rhythm that beckoned me to move. She reassured me, guiding me with her voice, and slowly, my cautious movements grew resolute. Our laughter transformed my small, darkened world into a realm of light and freedom. In those moments, the confines of my limitations vanished, replaced by the boundless expanse of shared joy. This journey, filled with support and acceptance, taught me that even in the darkest times, we can find light and meaning through the connections we cherish.

"To confront a powerful darkness, you must call up a greater power from within yourself."

~ Clarissa Pinkola Estés

chapter four

EMBRACING SHADOW

The dry season on the Caribbean coast of Costa Rica has always been my favorite. I love swimming in the inviting waters of the clear blue sea at this particular time, when there are no currents. I can swim calmly for hours, alternating between active movement and complete surrender to the ocean as I float on my back. I love to swim so long and far that I can't hear or see any more people. I feel as if I am in the womb again, so peaceful and connected as I'm transported far away into an underwater universe. Even when I could not see the sea, it kept me literally and figuratively afloat, returning me to the joy I held deep inside, regardless of outside circumstances. It reminded me, again and again, to let go and recall that connection. It's my favorite place in the entire world.

I have always felt this deep connection to the sea. It's the place I call home, where I feel safe to simply be. I experience exponential joy just by floating there, allowing my mind to relax and my body to let go of any tension. Throughout my two-year process of living with limited eyesight, I often found support for my waves of emotion in the waves of the ocean. I love the sensation of the water on my skin as I dive deep under the sea to hear the silence, coming back to the surface to breathe fully. It is a sensation of power and bliss.

One day during this season, I went for a sunset swim at Punta Uva, my favorite beach. The boys were playing in the sand, and I was far out in the ocean, feeling at home as usual. As I emerged from my swim, my eldest son asked for my goggles, and I said no, explaining that they were precious goggles and that, without them, I wouldn't be able to swim anymore, as my eyes were too sensitive to the salty water. He insisted, however, and I ended up agreeing to let him try them out. After a short time, I called to him, "Come out now, and give me my goggles." With fear in his voice, he said, "I'm sorry, Mum, they fell. I can't find them."

In disbelief, I had a total meltdown. "I told you!" I screamed. "I told you I didn't want to give them to you, and you insisted. I knew you'd lose them."

I was mostly upset with myself for not listening to my intuition and for giving in to my nine-year-old son. Then I started to cry. I cried and cried; I couldn't stop. I sat on the beach and just wept. I didn't have my sunglasses with me, and now I didn't have my goggles, and the light of the sun was hurting my eyes.

While my son ran to get my sunglasses for me, I stood up and went back to the sea. I stood there with the waves hitting my knees, tears still in my eyes, and said firmly to the sea, "You give me back my goggles right now! I can't be without them. Bring them back, please."

Suddenly, another wave arrived, and I felt the goggles touching my ankles. I bent down, took them in my hand, and said to the ocean, "Thank you. Thank you for giving me back what was mine."

I went back to the shore and sat there, still crying. Even with my goggles returned to me, the emotions I held were too much for me to process. It was as if the incident had opened a whole wailing part of me that was just waiting for the occasion to be expressed, for the proper space to be held.

My son sat next to me, trying to calm me down. "Mum, you got the goggles back. Why are you still like this?" he asked.

I told him I just couldn't stop, that I needed to cry. It was all the tension I had around my eyes. "It has nothing to do with you, my love," I explained. "I am so grateful that the sea gave me back my goggles, but I can't stop weeping. I wish it could also give me back my eyesight." And my sweet son just sat there with me, holding my hand while I cried. In the midst of it all, I still felt blessed to be held.

When I went back to the water, in a sense, I was

going back to that deeper connection I felt I had with the sea, asking it to allow me back into joy and release by returning the goggles, without which I couldn't swim. It was as if the sea had somehow wanted me back as well. Beyond my gratitude for getting my goggles back and the meaning I assigned to the experience, I became aware of how much I was holding on to my emotions. I realized that I had been "faking it" by keeping up a façade of strength. I hadn't been allowing any space for the part of me that was devastated by the loss of my eyesight, that felt so victimized by the whole situation. Outwardly, I was living the experience of a "strong" woman, not wanting to encourage feelings of pity from those around me, but, inside, there was another story.

What many call the "dark night of the soul," I prefer to call the "dark night of the ego." The soul always knows its light and path, but it is the ego that struggles to maintain appearances. I realized how I was playing out these dynamics of power and control in my interactions. I noticed how many of my relationships were based on universal archetypes, namely the savior and the victim archetypes, and the victim wasn't ever a role I liked. I didn't like hearing "victim stories" from other people, nor did I wish to show up as such. Perhaps my resistance to this representation of the savior archetype came from being born Palestinian in Israel, surrounded by the competition of suffering and victimhood. In such competitions, each party denies the victimhood and even the existence, the essence, of the other.

I had been so determined not to fall into the "poor me" victim role, but, in doing so, I ended up ignoring my own needs, minimizing my pain, suppressing my vulnerability, and refusing the support I actually required. I had been equating asking for help with weakness and constantly pushed myself to keep functioning, even when it was harmful. I had downplayed what was happening, presented a façade of resilience, and focused on sharing primarily my moments of strength and success, while leaving my own struggles largely unspoken, even to myself.

At the same time, the experience stripped me of my familiar role of the rescuer, the one who fixes, supports, and holds everything together, and letting go of that identity was painful. I had been raised with a deep sense of guilt and obligation, and being the one who cared for others had always made me feel safe and in control. The rescuer role had been my trauma response, my way of managing chaos by staying needed. So I coped by hiding.

In reality, I was swimming in uncertainty, in the unknown. I continued to ruminate on the same questions: *Will I ever get my eyesight back? Is this just an experience for me to learn a lesson, and then all will go back to normal?* Despite the progress I had made, I felt exhausted by the endless process. I was constantly waiting for the healing to be over.

Time and again, I would convince myself, "This is the final stage." That is what I told myself after the surgery, and again after a month had passed, and again after another, and then again after a whole trimester had come and gone. But the healing kept evolving, with no clear endpoint in sight. Desperation consumed me as I longed to return to normalcy. I tried to find comfort in the reminders that returning to normalcy was what we had all been seeking, ever since the pandemic. The concept of "normal" had become elusive, and we all shared a pervasive sense of helplessness and hopelessness, even if it wasn't openly acknowledged.

In my desire, obsession, and desperation to heal, I didn't allow the process to unfold naturally. Every encounter, healing session, and potential breakthrough felt like it could finally be the missing piece in my recovery, a dance of one step forward and two steps back that plodded on for an entire year. All the while, my personal struggles seemed to be mirrored by the collective, for whom each new Covid strain meant plunging once more into uncertainty and fear.

I tried to communicate hope and trust, holding on to my heart's guidance to keep going as normal, but I realized how deeply depressed and abandoned I felt. In all the meditations and talks I was listening to, the message was clear: move away from the negative and focus on positive, peaceful feelings. Even though I, too, believed in that message, all I could feel was sadness, anger, and frustration in response to the claims that we needed to focus on light and love, that the shadows and darkness haunting us were of our own making.

Symbolically, we are all reaching for the light. But, as I began to realize that instability had become my norm, I came to find unexpected comfort and a strange sense of safety in darkness. My physical experience kept bringing me down to earth, where the light hurt my eyes and the darkness soothed them. Darkness didn't scare me—it held me. It was familiar, quiet, even soothing, and it mirrored the inner landscape I knew so well. Having spent much of my life living and working in conflict zones, I had learned to navigate crises and chaos with ease. The light, in fact, was at times unbearably harsh and exposing. I had once felt nourished by the sun, but now I felt more comfortable when there was no light, no sun, and nothing around me. I could relax into it.

I received hope once again that I could heal my vision naturally when I listened to *You Are the Placebo* and *Becoming Supernatural,* two books by Dr. Joe Dispenza, a well-known author, speaker, and researcher. His teachings often center around the idea of tapping into our innate potential and reprogramming our minds to create the reality we desire. In my meditations, I saw what Dr. Dispenza was referring to, entering fully into pure darkness, pure potentiality. One deep meditation brought me a vision that felt both symbolic and cellular. I saw particles of light—like photons—streaming from the sun and descending toward Earth. In that moment, I understood that we, too, originate from that light. As these particles reached the Earth's atmosphere, I saw them breaking apart, fragmenting into what I perceived as individual souls taking form.

The fracturing didn't feel violent; it felt necessary. It was as if the outer shell of pure light had to break open for us to become human—to take on matter, emotion, memory. Even our hearts, once whole in the realm of light, seemed to fracture slightly to make space for the full range of human experience: grief, longing, love, and compassion.

In that vision, becoming human was not a fall from grace, but a sacred process of condensation— of spirit-made matter, of light-made flesh. My vision (or rather lack thereof) was helping me align with his concepts of transcending the limitations of the physical self to access higher states of consciousness and potential. I had to shed the layers of ego and physicality to realize the true essence of my being—a luminous, interconnected part of the whole. My lack of outer vision served as a powerful metaphor for personal growth and the journey toward self-realization.

Once I saw this, "dancing in the dark" became my motto, my daily practice, and a place that held me tight throughout the process. I learned to dance with all of my parts, the ones in the shadows—angry, frustrated, annoyed, depressed, sad—and the ones in the light—compassionate, understanding, and *innersitting*. "Innersit" is a term that came to me when I was contemplating the word "understanding." I realized I did not want to "go under" or "stand" to understand, so I chose the words "inner" to replace "under" and "sitting" to replace "standing."

Thus, I came to "innersitting," an intriguing concept that plays on the idea of sitting inside oneself to find the answers within, rather than merely understanding externally. This approach emphasizes the importance of inner reflection, mindfulness, and connecting with one's true self to navigate life's challenges and decisions, encouraging individuals to cultivate a practice of stillness and self-awareness that facilitates personal growth and a deeper understanding of oneself and the world. The process of introspection and deep contemplation can lead to insights, clarity, and wisdom, which ultimately brought me to trust.

This innersitting dance kept me alive. I learned how to be with uncertainty and mingle with the dark and the unknown, allowing them to embrace me in a way I never had before. When I managed to temporarily let go of my need for certainty—a certain date for gaining my eyesight back, a certain action that would bring it back—and abandoned my expectation for things to be different from what they were, I was able to rest, sit back, and release control . . . at least for a few moments.

I could sense—though I couldn't see—that this state wasn't specific to me, but rather that it was common to all of us in the context of the planetary pandemic. We just weren't able to articulate it in those words, as we were too busy with the antagonizing polarities of who was right and who was wrong and whether the virus existed or was a matter of manipulation by a secret agenda. I would listen to different people and perspectives, but none of them resonated with my heart, and I was amazed by how heartless and out of focus the whole discussion was. *Where did the humans go? Where did the heart go?* There was no space between right and wrong or good and bad.

There's a well-loved line by Rumi that says, "Out beyond ideas of wrongdoing and rightdoing, there is a field. I'll meet you there." That field became a lifeline for me. In a world consumed by polarization and moral absolutism, I felt myself drawn to that space beyond judgment—where truth lives in nuance and hearts speak without needing to be right. I didn't want to leave that field. In fact, I couldn't. It was the only place I felt fully alive in the midst of darkness.

I said little, as I felt my energy would be wasted. Instead, I tried to offer space for people to speak from their hearts, rather than their minds. I invited vulnerability and authenticity, hoping to create a refuge from the noise, a space where people could share how lost they felt in the midst of this unfolding planetary crisis. Sometimes, it worked, and people dropped into something real and raw. But not always. Often, the pull of polarization was too strong.

The world had become so divided, so binary, that people felt pressured to pick a side, to be "right," to argue. In those moments, my invitations to speak from the heart were met with resistance, silence, or defensiveness. I found myself speechless and positionless—not because I lacked clarity, but because I no longer believed that clarity had to come in the form of taking sides. And that, for some, was incomprehensible.

Drawing from my twenty-two years of experience working in conflict zones, I knew that assigning blame often oversimplifies complex situations. In conflict, the truth is rarely black and white; it lies in how we navigate and resolve it. Conflict itself isn't inherently good or bad; it's our response that determines its outcome, ideally leading to mutual benefit for all parties involved. I didn't want to hold space for division or reinforcing polarity, so I invented a protocol to support the people around me. I would start all my meetings with a prayer and say the following words:

"I invite us all to take a moment to connect with our hearts and set aside our analytical minds. Let's approach this conversation with open hearts, listening deeply to each other's experiences and perspectives. Remember, this is a space free from judgment or opinions; it's about sharing our truths and connecting on a deeper level. Thank you for being here and for your willingness to engage in this way."

In spite of the instabilities and unexpected changes I had faced over the years, I still wanted to have the significance I used to have in the world, to be defined by the amazing things I did. I wanted to mean something, yet I felt I no longer did. I was alone in my world, and the few interactions I could have were in the dark. I juggled my multiple identities, sometimes with joy and sometimes with a great sense of challenge. This paradox wasn't a dichotomy, but rather life's essential complexity at its best.

I also wanted to start repaying all those who had supported me financially, emotionally, and logistically since I lost my sight. The need to give something back was beginning to feel immediate, even though I was still going through the healing process. I couldn't seem to let go and receive fully, too afraid that it would make me feel or appear weak. Giving back made me feel like less of a failure; it made me feel significant and equal again.

I accomplished these needs in January 2021 by opening up Dancing in the Dark to other people through public movement events. By then, I had accepted the reality that I might never see again, yet I was still desperate to return to normal life and connect with a broader community beyond my jungle life. In the safe space of this forum, I publicly and authentically shared my vulnerability, allowing myself to release some of the internal pressure I had carried.

These were sacred spaces to be together and explore what it meant to be in the darkness, to dance among uncertainty and the unknown. They became my way to come back to life and interact with the outside world from a different place, a place of making even instability feel okay. In this place, we could all speak or dance about what was going on within us, where we could be simultaneously in the world and not in the world. It fulfilled my need to take action and contribute, providing a comforting illusion that I was still just as able to be meaningful and of service as I ever was.

This was my way of taking responsibility for and constructively dealing with my feelings of powerlessness since losing my eyesight. Being vulnerable meant loving myself enough to express my feelings before they overwhelmed me, something I had struggled with for my entire life due to my conditioning. I had thought I needed my attitude of strength, and I held on to that act so as not to worsen my self-pity. I wanted to feel like the agent and creator of my life, rather than a victim of my circumstances. At the same time, I so wanted to believe that all this experience might have— *must* have—a higher purpose. It *had* to be for something bigger, right? I needed to give higher meaning to what was going on for me at an individual level. The ego plays such games.

The ego, often stigmatized, plays a crucial role in our psychological survival, especially during challenging childhoods. But is its role merely a survival tactic, or is there a deeper strategy ingrained in our lives? Throughout my journey, I've contemplated these questions, such as whether there is a meaningful distinction between the ego and learned survival tactics. Without the ego's protective mechanisms, navigating adversity and maintaining a sense of self-worth would have been immensely difficult, if not impossible. I believe that acknowledging this complexity allows us to appreciate how the ego, despite its stigma, has been instrumental in our resilience and survival.

From an early age, I internalized the notion that my worth was tied to my achievements. And, growing up in a patriarchal society, this belief was reinforced at every turn. I learned that, to be valued, I had to excel, to outshine, to prove my competence and worth through visible accomplishments. This core belief became a survival mechanism, a way to navigate a world that often undervalues and undermines.

On one level, this belief served me well. It propelled me to strive for excellence, to push boundaries, and to achieve goals that brought external recognition. In a world where the contributions of women and marginalized voices are frequently overlooked, my drive to accomplish became both a shield and a sword. It allowed me to carve out a space for myself, to assert my presence and capabilities, but it also came at a cost.

The relentless focus on accomplishment narrowed my vision of who I could be, confining my sense of self to the roles and achievements listed on my résumé. By equating my worth with my productivity, I lost touch with the deeper, intrinsic value that lies within. My identity became fragmented, splintered by the pressures to conform to external expectations.

As I embarked on my journey of self-discovery in the dark, I began to see the limitations of these core beliefs. I saw how they were rooted in survival, born out of necessity in a world that demanded proof of worth. I saw that, in clinging to them, I had overlooked the wholeness that existed beyond what I could accomplish. I realized that true self-awareness required embracing all the parts of myself—the light and the dark, the accomplished and the vulnerable.

Maybe the greater meaning of this whole experience was to let go of my constant inner dialogue, to drop the belief that who I am is determined by what I accomplish. These core beliefs are what had helped me survive, but they ultimately limited my ability to touch my wholeness. By recognizing the role this belief had played in my life, I could appreciate its function without being confined by it. It had helped me survive and even thrive in a patriarchal world, but it was not the full measure of who I am.

As it turned out, letting go of these beliefs didn't mean dismissing my achievements. Rather, it meant expanding my understanding of self to include my innate worth, which was fully independent of external validation. Meanwhile, the more I spoke about Dancing in the Dark, the less I was dancing alone. I began facilitating sacred cacao dance rituals during retreats—preparing the cacao with care, creating soundscapes from eclectic music, and inviting others to open their hearts through movement. I needed the presence of others to dance again. Even if I couldn't see their faces or read their expressions, I longed for connection, and their energy held me.

Giving back made me feel useful and needed—but it also kept me from surrendering to the stillness I truly craved. The experience was both liberating and frustrating. It reminded me I could still be of service and create beauty, even in the dark. But it also showed me that, underneath, I was still bypassing my own needs. I was offering healing while still raw and unhealed, holding space for others before I had fully held space for myself. It took me a long time to realize that, sometimes, the most radical act of service is not to lead others, but to sit in the dark with myself and do nothing at all.

In my personal journey, I have often fallen into the pattern of bypassing the essential lesson of learning how to receive by over-giving and anticipating others' needs. Like many women, I gave excessively, not solely out of pure generosity, but to feel needed and to derive a sense of worth. This over-giving was my way of avoiding my own vulnerabilities and the discomfort of receiving.

I realized that this dynamic created a cycle where my dismissal of my own needs and desires led to feelings of resentment and depletion. The act of giving to others masked the need to feel useful and necessary, which concealed a deeper fear that I was unworthy of receiving unconditional love and support. It was a form of self-betrayal, sidelining my true needs in favor of fulfilling others' expectations. And it wasn't until I was forced to receive rather than give that I was able to see this.

When I began cultivating a strong sense of self-worth and self-acceptance, not as a concept, but as a lived practice during my healing journey, everything started to shift. This wasn't something that happened overnight. It began quietly in the moments when I allowed myself to receive care without guilt, in the pauses where I chose rest over performance.

The shift felt unnatural after a life built on giving and being useful, competent, and in control. But as my eyesight faded and my external roles dissolved, I was forced to face the deeper truth: for years, I had been outsourcing my worth to my doing, not my being. Now, I had to meet myself without titles, without visibility, without the validation that had once sustained me.

Learning to receive without conditions or apology was the threshold. It taught me that worth is not transactional. It's inherent. And the more I honored that in myself, the more I could extend that recognition to others.

Embracing my own worthiness and learning to receive wasn't just a personal shift; it changed how I related to the world around me. When I stopped over-giving and began honoring my own needs, I realized something powerful: I could no longer pretend to be self-sufficient. I had to acknowledge my interdependence, not just with those like me but with those who were radically different from me.

This shift created more room for diversity, not just in theory but in lived experience. Because when we believe we must have all the answers or carry everything alone, we tend to surround ourselves with sameness—people who reflect back what we already know or feel safe with. But when we allow ourselves to receive, we open to the possibility that others—different in background, belief, or way of being—have something we need. We allow ourselves to acknowledge that we have something to learn.

Receiving is an act of humility. It's an acknowledgment that I am not whole without relationship, that my healing is not separate from yours. That's where diversity becomes not just inclusion—but mutual transformation.

Reflecting, this process taught me that there is a fine line between being a victim, complaining, "Why me?" and being vulnerable, sharing authentically about our difficulties. Once I was able to release the judgments I had about my situation and needing help, moving away from my undercover victim status, I understood that vulnerability takes strength. It took me an immense amount of courage to feel my own emotions authentically and to let people in, sometimes those I didn't even know. In my heart, I knew that the only way out was in ... and out again.

What I came to understand is that healing isn't

about returning to who we were. It's about allowing who we truly are to emerge, often through the very experiences we've tried to avoid. I had to face the parts of myself I had long buried, the grief, the rage, the vulnerability, the need. These were my shadows. And the more I turned toward them instead of away, the more I discovered that the shadow is not our enemy— it is our teacher. It reveals the places we are still divided within, the places still waiting for love.

Embracing the shadow doesn't mean getting lost in despair. It means acknowledging the full spectrum of our humanity, our contradictions, our fragility, our beauty. And it means trusting that even in the dark, there is intelligence. There is a purpose. There is life.

This is the paradox of healing: the darkness that I feared would swallow me became the ground that held me. It stripped away the illusion. It redefined connection. And it opened the way for a new kind of vision— one that sees through the eyes of the soul.

"*Everything can be taken from a man but one thing: the last of human freedoms—to choose one's attitude in any given set of circumstances, to choose one's way.*"

~ *Viktor E. Frankl*

chapter five

SURRENDER TO THE SOUL

When my eyes, what we call the windows to the soul, stopped working, I took it as an invitation from my soul for me to look inside and make peace with her, allowing her the full expression that she had not received to date. If I could sum up my entire experience of this healing journey in one phrase, it would be "getting together with my soul." This is a story that connects me deeply to my essence. If you have ever lost and found that connection, you know exactly what I mean.

Through these experiences, trusting the process has taken on a new dimension, prompting reflection on what has opened up within me and what might be opening up for us all collectively. These profound disruptions have the potential to unearth hidden strengths, resilience, and new perspectives that can lead to personal and societal growth.

For years, I had been simultaneously living in full uncertainty and resisting the uncertainty. I was drowning in pain, yet trying so hard to disconnect from the pain and the fear that I would never see again. And still, I had to learn, I had to trust, I had to surrender. When there was no more hope, I had to find hope in the stillness of my heart and the vision of myself in the future.

I had done a lot of work with my inner child before, but this time, it wasn't the child in me that needed attention. It was the future self I hadn't yet become. I needed her to hold me. I needed her to remind me that there was more life still ahead, beyond the dark.

I learned to be present with uncertainty and cling not to answers, but to a felt sense of trust—trust in my soul. In one of my meditations, I saw her clearly: tall, grounded, graceful. Her long hair moved freely in the wind, and there was a light in her eyes that I could not yet access in myself. She didn't flinch in the face of pain. She wasn't trying to escape. She stood in her truth with quiet power, and she saw me. That vision kept me going.

She became my compass. She carried the wisdom I couldn't yet remember. In the depths of my grief, I imagined her breathing with me, her calm presence steadying my trembling. She was the air I was breathing. Every time I connected with her, I felt a little less alone in the dark, knowing she had already made it through.

Blindness brought me to a new place of heart-centered navigation, teaching me to trust this inner compass I had. I realized the only thing I could really hold on to was how I felt in each moment, each interaction. So, I tried to stay within and listen deeply to my heart, the only thing I seemed capable of grasping onto and feeling in control of. I chose to put my authenticity and vulnerability at the core of my healing process. Was my heart in contraction or expansion? Did it feel good or bad? Through heart-centered navigation, I learned to find a new normal in the chaos and uncertainty, just as the world had learned to adapt to the ever-changing landscape of the pandemic.

In the fall of 2021, I realized how much I was craving solitude and movement, away from my family, at my own pace and in my own space. I yearned for this space desperately, feeling unable to handle any more interactions or explanations. I simply didn't want to talk. I longed for silence and peace of mind, to be alone with my thoughts. I wanted to be alone in our Caribbean jungle house for just enough time to conduct my own silent retreat and dive deep into my being.

I asked my partner for this space, and he graciously obliged, taking the kids to the other house we were purchasing in the Pacific and giving me ten days to myself in the jungle. I prepared for the silent retreat, promising myself not to engage with anyone and truly honor this time for deep connection and reflection. It was time to be alone with my sadness.

Once I was truly alone, without any distractions, I was able to see that I felt deeply depressed. It had been almost two years since I had lost my eyesight, and a year since the surgery that was meant to restore it. Now, the doctors were suggesting another operation—another risk, another uncertainty, another invitation for hope without guarantee. I wasn't ready. I couldn't bear the thought of another setback.

Even my anger had abandoned me. What remained beneath it was grief—raw, vast, and hollow. I grieved not just the loss of sight, but the life I used to live: the independence, the spontaneous social gatherings, the simplicity of walking down a street without assistance. All of that was gone. And, strangely, I had lost the will to care anymore. I didn't want to fight. I didn't want to explain. I just wanted to disappear. Something in me had collapsed.

So I let myself hide. The jungle house—tucked away in the trees, wrapped in birdsong and mist—became my cocoon. I would sit in silence for hours, letting the grief wash over me. Tears came without my needing to understand them. As the sadness moved through my body like a storm that had no sense of schedule, all I could do was breathe.

Nature saved me during this period of my life. I

couldn't see, but I could touch, smell, and hear. I would go to the trees in the garden and hug them, feeling their energy connect with my spirit. I would sit on the earth and cry, asking, praying, and waiting for it to end. Then, a gentle breeze of a whisper would come to my ears:

It's all going to be fine. Love is all around you; just feel it. Relax, breathe, and feel us. We are here with you. You don't need to see us—just feel us.

And I could. Once I let go of the need to see with my eyes, I could see what was invisible. I heard the voices from elsewhere, and the sense of being trapped dissipated. Then, slowly, I began to notice something: the more I continued resisting the darkness, the more it softened. It wasn't trying to destroy me. It was trying to be seen.

This is how I began to embrace the grief—not by fixing it or rushing it, but by making space for it to exist. I stopped pretending I was okay. I stopped performing resilience. I allowed myself to fall apart in the arms of the jungle, and somehow, in that falling, I began to feel presence, and that was the beginning.

Rethinking everything about my identity, particularly in the context of losing and rediscovering my connection to myself and my soul, was a deeply transformative journey. As I reflect on these times, a mix of sensations arises in my body even now. There's a sense of release, as if shedding old layers, and also a profound stillness, as if finding a deeper peace within. It was a journey marked by vulnerability and courage, where each moment of introspection and acceptance led to a greater sense of authenticity and alignment with my true self.

The potential hidden within such experiences lies in our ability to adapt, learn, and grow from adversity, to forge deeper connections with ourselves and others and create a more compassionate and inclusive world. Collectively, these kinds of disruptions invite us to question our established norms and beliefs, encouraging a reevaluation of what truly matters in our lives. They challenge us to face uncertainty and change with openness and flexibility. Trusting the process means embracing the unknown with faith in our capacity to navigate challenges and emerge stronger, both individually and together.

It was through the stillness of my silent retreat that I truly learned to give in to the quiet acceptance of what was. That surrender gave me the strength to face what I had been avoiding. And so, I decided to do the surgery.

My second surgery took place a year and a half after the first. When the day came, my body was filled with fear. This time, I wanted to go alone. I was committed to rejecting all of the support I was offered until my partner, with his experience and skill as a therapist, was finally able to break down my defense mechanisms by articulating to me what was going on and how afraid I was of feeling defeated again. I eventually admitted that I was terrified of waking up after the surgery and not being able to see at all.

Once again, I came out of the operating room with my eyes covered to protect them until the follow-up appointment. The next morning, we went to the doctor. I was terrified to open my eyes; if there was no improvement once again, I knew I would be devastated. But when he checked my eyes, the doctor declared the surgery a success. I was finally ready to see again.

He was right. It was not full sight yet, but it was clearer and brighter, and I could see far. It was different, whether I liked it or not. I couldn't see close up, but I was given special glasses that would allow me to do things like read and drive. I could finally get back in the driver's seat of my life (and my car).

Still, I was afraid to accept this reality. I was scared to admit that I could see, that the light didn't hurt me, and that I could keep my eyes open. It took me an entire day and night to reassure myself that it was safe to see, to let go of the identity of dependence and weakness that had clung to me. Over the past two years, my identity as the dependent person who couldn't see had become so ingrained that I couldn't even entertain the possibility of regaining my sight and what that might mean.

This experience made me reflect deeply on the concept of safety. Much like my journey to accept my restored vision, people worldwide were facing the challenge of shedding the layers of protection they had grown accustomed to. I would have to reassure myself that it was safe to see again, just as many people were navigating similar feelings of vulnerability as they moved out of the COVID-19 pandemic. Taking off masks, returning to work, and re-engaging with the world required them to let go of a protective identity they had adopted during the crisis.

This kind of transition involves overcoming fears and uncertainties, both physical and emotional. For me, it was about trusting that it was safe to move forward, to reconnect with others and embrace a new reality after a period of profound change. The parallel between my experience and the collective's underscores the universal struggle of adapting to new circumstances. It takes courage to step into the light after a long period of darkness.

Every time it seemed like I was accepting my circumstances, life would give me another opportunity to see how I wasn't fully surrendering. Some part of me would fight back, reasserting its demands and expectations because I was still attached to things happening a certain way. All along, I had hoped that doctors' visits would bring good news about my eyesight; or that a cleanse might clear up blockages in my digestive system, thus influencing my third eye; or that, somewhere out there, there might be some magic pill—whatever that was. These possibilities had continued to keep my hopes high.

That's the thing about surrender: it doesn't last. A decade prior, I had taught a course called *Surrender to the Spirit Within* in Topanga, California. Now, in Costa Rica, I was realizing that I didn't actually have a clue what surrender meant. I was still waiting for a miracle.

It wasn't until there was nothing more to do and nowhere else to go that I finally surrendered. I kept that reality in mind while still trying to do things and go places. Praying for grace and letting go of figuring out the what, the how, and the why ultimately saved me. When there was nothing else to do, I had to face the deep sorrow, the deep sadness, and all the other feelings I had been pushing down in an effort to stay positive and confident in my healing process. Finally, I surrendered to myself, to my heart.

Surrender is not about giving up. Surrender is about letting go—completely—of any expectation, hope, or waiting for anything. What can save us from the tendency to seek control over our lives is faith in ourselves and the universe that, whatever the outcome is, it will be good for us. Whatever happens, it will be okay. There is no need to control, plan, organize, prioritize, or even *do* any of the tasks that we are programmed to do our entire lives, beginning with our first years in school.

Surrender is also about flowing with nature, observing its pace, and understanding that there is nowhere to go and nothing to do. We can experience what is happening without judgment and choose to give it meaning that feels supportive to us in whatever we are going through.

I am so grateful that my surgeries worked. I am so grateful for what I can see, although at times, I still wondered what really happened. I couldn't control much about my eyesight loss, but I could control the meaning I assigned to the experience. I could tell myself that my soul had chosen this; otherwise, I wouldn't have experienced it. We are spiritual beings having human experiences, and my human experience included two years of blindness and the ensuing deep dive into my interior castle, as Caroline Myss would refer to it. Part of this process has been all of the support, love, and humility it brought me—and that is the story I want to share.

I moved through the depths of grief, through the feelings of being a victim of something cruel and senseless. At my core, I wasn't a victim. I was a participant in a transformation that I hadn't chosen but was being asked to meet with presence. What shifted wasn't a rejection of the feelings; it was the recognition that I didn't have to stay there.

Instead of seeing the loss I experienced as something that had happened *to* me, I began to sense it was happening *for* or *with* me. There was an intelligence to it, a deeper unfolding I couldn't yet fully grasp. The question in my heart was no longer, "Why is this happening?" but, "Why now, in this moment, when everything else in the world seems to be unraveling too?"

Once I saw that surrender was not the same as defeat, I understood that it was actually an act of trust. It was an opportunity to lean into something greater than my immediate comprehension and trust that there was meaning beyond my own articulation, that perhaps I was being prepared for something I hadn't imagined. That question—*Why now?*—was less about seeking an answer and more about trusting in a deeper rhythm. It wasn't about giving up, but giving *in*, softening and listening rather than resisting what was.

I started to reclaim my agency in partnership with whatever was happening, which meant living with the loss, not against it. This shift in perspective changed everything. It allowed me to respond rather than react to what was being asked of me and shaped how I spoke, how I related to others, and how I created.

Surrender became my entry point into presence. It provided a way of walking with pain and possibility in the same breath. A new kind of vision began to emerge, one that didn't rely on sight, but on something much deeper: attunement to the unseen, the unspoken soul of things. The two years of my healing journey taught me the true meaning of surrender and letting go. All of my certainty had gone out the window. But such was the case for the whole planet. Just as I questioned my path and the reasons behind my loss of sight, many people around the world were looking back on the COVID-19 pandemic and wondering, Did that really happen? Did we, as a global community, really dive that deeply into our own interior castles during periods of lockdowns and isolation?

During the global lockdowns, some people checked

out, became depressed in confinement, and stayed within, stuck in mourning of the old ways and of what they knew as "normal." Others thrived, taking the rare chance to slow down or focus on online businesses or homesteading, finding new ways to flourish amidst uncertainty. And tragically, others passed to the next realm of reality that isn't ours. The significance we attribute to transformations like these is what determines how they shape our lives.

The polarities that existed before the pandemic are still present, and in many cases, they have deepened. The process of re-engaging with the world has been fraught with uncertainty and fear, much like my hesitation in accepting my restored vision. It wasn't just my eyesight I was unsure of—it was life itself. Who *was* I now? Who was I allowed to become, now that I could no longer lead with the same certainty, the same visibility, the same "functionality" I once took for granted?

During a trip to Israel in April 2023, I observed these universal reflections firsthand. People were grappling with their experiences, seeking meaning in the challenges they had faced, and trying to reconcile their personal growth with the ongoing divisions in the world. We were all trying to embrace our new realities.

Looking back, I see how each unraveling has led me closer to truth. Not the kind of truth that shouts answers, but the kind that sits quietly in the soul, waiting to be remembered. I no longer see the darkness as something to escape, but as a sacred teacher.

It stripped away illusions I didn't know I was carrying and returned me to what is essential. I learned to listen differently and see with more than my eyes, trusting in what was unseen and living from the inside out. I was no longer rushing to fix, prove, or become. Instead, I could just *be*—gently and fully.

Life is sacred, and so is everything that relates to it. This includes me. My life, body, and spirit are sacred. I feel truly blessed to be living where I am right now and to have experienced what I have experienced. It might sound strange to say I feel blessed to have lost my vision for two years, but despite the frustrations and disappointments, I came to feel it was a gift. When we are shown a unique opportunity to dive deep inside our souls and come out with a whole new vision of life, we must be willing to see it.

"Feminine power isn't something we go out and acquire; it's already within us. It's something we become willing to experience. Something to admit we have."

~ Marianne Williamson

chapter six

RECLAIMING FEMININE POWER

True feminine power is not about control, perfection, or independence at any cost. It's about vulnerability, interdependence, and allowing ourselves to be seen, supported, and carried when we can't do it alone. Motherhood had already begun to crack that open for me, revealing how unsustainable the myth of the self-sufficient woman truly is. Because being a mother demands everything—and yet, we are so often expected to do it in isolation. We celebrate the mother who sacrifices, who never asks and carries it all herself. But true motherhood, I came to learn, is not about martyrdom. It's about modeling wholeness, which includes the courage to need, the wisdom to ask, and the grace to receive.

Losing my sight is what made this lesson undeniable. I had no choice but to lean on others, surrendering the illusion of self-reliance and discovering a deeper strength that was rooted not in doing it all, but in being fully present with what is. The process led me home to a new kind of leadership, a new way of mothering, and a more embodied expression of power that grows in circles, softness, and shared breath.

Just as losing my sight was a catalyst for my own introspection, teaching me to rely on inner vision rather than physical sight, it greatly influenced my approach to motherhood. No longer just a role defined by visible actions and tangible achievements, motherhood, too, became a journey of inner surrender and acceptance. I found a deeper understanding of my role as a mother, wherein nurturing became as much about inner growth and self-connection as it was about external care.

Becoming a mother didn't just awaken a primal force within me—it redefined the core of how I understood womanhood, value, and power. After decades of working as a gender advisor, advocating for women's rights and inclusion in peace building and leadership, I was stunned to realize how little value society truly places on motherhood, the very root of life itself. In the spaces where I worked, outward expressions of agency were celebrated—titles, visibility, and measurable achievements—while the invisible labor of caregiving and the emotional intelligence required to raise a child were treated as if they belonged to a lesser realm.

Given this societal underpinning, it makes sense that I once thought my highest potential would be something outside of me, something out there in the ether that I could aspire to embody or become. Little did I know that my highest potential was actually hidden deep within me. Then, at the age of thirty-eight (and again at forty), I gave birth naturally to a healthy child at home, just before sunset, to the sound of the howler monkeys in the trees and the waves of the ocean. It had never struck me before that respect for motherhood and women is intrinsically linked to respect for Mother Nature. I had to cross that threshold myself to understand: the devaluation of motherhood is not separate from the global crisis women face. In fact, it is at the heart of the crisis. When the most life-giving aspects of womanhood are dismissed, when nurturing and emotional labor are treated as less valuable, we create the conditions for violence, economic inequality, and spiritual disconnection to thrive.

The birth of my babies was also the birth of myself as a mother and a creator, and it brought me back to something ancient and unshakable. It reconnected me to a power beyond intellect or effort—a power rooted in the body and in trust. But birth was only the beginning. My sense of self, my relationship to time, my priorities, and my understanding of purpose all rearranged themselves around this new life.

In motherhood, I had to slow down, listen more

deeply, and learn to be with uncertainty in a way I never had before. In that process, I came to understand motherhood not just as a role but as a spiritual path. One that requires presence, resilience, and deep humility. I learned my deepest layers of patience, resiliency, and resourcefulness, even in the darkest of moments. Perhaps most importantly, I learned the crucial roles of sisterhood and reclaiming feminine power, two aspects that are intimately connected.

To prepare for my first delivery, my husband and I left New York, where we were living at the time, and rented a house on the Pacific Coast of Costa Rica. The house had a pool overlooking the ocean and jungle, and a beautiful garden full of flowers. We arrived there a month before the birth, or so we thought. I had my birthday celebration a week after our arrival, and my gift was my baby—just four days later! Perhaps it was the daily 5Rhythms dancing I was doing with my partner, our bodies still echoing the beat that first united us on a dusty dance floor at Burning Man in 2008.

"The 5Rhythms" is a movement meditation practice created by Gabrielle Roth in the late 1970s. It is a form of ecstatic dance that allows participants to express themselves through five different movement styles or rhythms: Flow, Staccato, Chaos, Lyrical, and Stillness. Each rhythm represents a different energy and emotion, and participants are encouraged to explore and move through these rhythms in a free and spontaneous way. The practice is often done as a group, with participants moving together in a non-judgmental and supportive environment. For my husband and me, the experience was like twin flames finding their way through movement before language, dancing life into form.

I delivered by water birth with just him and a local medicine woman. Our midwife didn't make it on time, and since this was our first baby, we felt that a woman who had given birth could be of help without burdening us with her presence or any unnecessary advice. For both my partner and me, this birth was about us and the baby; we wanted to be the only ones experiencing that initial connection. We felt it was a rite of passage, an empowering moment for us as a couple and a spiritual experience for us as a family, welcoming our baby in privacy.

The night before the birth, we were getting ready to go out dancing again, but I decided to stay home while he went out. I was happy to stay by myself, connecting to the surrounding nature, the darkness, and the wildness of the jungle. Then I started to feel a strong pressure in my lower back. When my husband came back home after midnight, he massaged my lower back to calm me down, and we went to sleep holding each other lovingly. When I woke up in the morning, I lay there, wondering how the day would unfold, enjoying the sunrise and the beautiful view, the birds singing, and the monkeys howling.

When my son's time had arrived, it was a moment

of total surrender to the power of Spirit, God, Energy, Nature, or whatever one calls the force that supported me while I was giving birth. It felt like I had to die to give birth. The pain was intense, but I had to let go of any temptation to rationalize or analyze, temporarily severing contact with the outside world. Drifting within, I connected to nature, breathed in unison with the howler monkeys that echoed in the distance, and disappeared, only to reappear with a baby coming through my body.

In the end, the birth of my son was the scariest, most amazing, and most empowering event I have ever experienced. My body's ability to expand, develop, and carry a whole new being stunned me. My power of creation was beyond my capacity for understanding. That truth was suddenly undeniably clear and potent.

Since then, the journey has been toward understanding that power. I see how our society ignores and fears the mother's inherent power to create and educate children. Through childbirth, I learned—or rediscovered—how powerful I was, yet also how scared I was to acknowledge my power. It was as if recognizing it would take away the power of my partner, my family, and my society.

We women often internalize this fear, unconsciously or consciously apologizing for our power. We have betrayed our power of creation, ignoring, rejecting, and abandoning it to such an extent that we don't even remember we once had it. And, when memories of our power arise, they appear as shadows from the past, constantly competing with male dominance. We seem to think that, in order to regain our power, we must either destroy or imitate others. I truly believe that is why our society is the way it is.

Pregnant women, birthing mothers, and mothers are all under a mental occupation in our society. There is little respect for them as creators, and we allocate the power of birthing to male-dominated institutions and male doctors who have no inherent understanding of how a woman's body works. They don't understand what it means to give birth, yet they are so often the ones in control, telling women how to birth and mother their children.

No, I say. Our power is ours alone, regardless of what, where, or who we are. Our power is deeply, honestly, and fully ours and has nothing to do with anyone but us. Yet, fearful of its vast capacity, we undermine it. We can deny it, ignore it, or reject it, but that doesn't mean it isn't there. So why are we scared?

I believe that the feminine power we all hold within us (men and women) has been pushed to the side by centuries of patriarchy, which has taught us that to be feminine is to be submissive, to be a woman is to be taken care of, and to be vulnerable is to be weak. Somehow, we have all internalized this patriarchal system and pushed aside beautiful feminine values that our society perceives as less than. Less than what? Less than masculine values.

No longer wanting to accommodate the status quo perception of women as the fragile, weaker gender, I reclaimed my power as a woman, a mother, and a being beyond measure. I had to learn to accept my power and live from within it, rather than believing it was something I had to fight for. When we come from a place of knowing we have our power, there is no need to fight for it or wait for someone else to give it to us. This is true for all women, whether or not they choose to be mothers or give birth, and relates to the status of human evolution itself.

We can only evolve by expanding our humanity, and birth is the ultimate action that allows us to do so. Without birth, humanity ceases to exist. This power of creation, shared by men and women as it requires two beings to come together to create a third, has been so dismissed, disregarded, and diminished by our patriarchal society, which grants dominance to some over others. From partners in creation, we humans—women and men—have become adversaries.

To reclaim our inherent power in recognizing the undeniable significance of creation, we must first recognize how deeply these divisive constructs are woven into our personal, cultural, and collective narratives. My own life has been marked by fault lines—between identities, geographies, and belief systems. I was born into conflict and spent decades working in its aftermath. But over time, I've come to see that the real work is not just about ending war or resolving disputes; it's about transforming the inner architecture that keeps us locked in separation. Whether in peace building between nations or within the intimate spaces of family and self, the path forward begins with our willingness to bridge with others, at times reimagining what it means to belong—to ourselves, to one another, and to something greater than the stories we've inherited.

It was in this context that I encountered the Gene Keys, a system of living wisdom rooted in the I Ching, astrology, and human design. They are not a fixed belief system, but rather a contemplative path to unlock the hidden potential within our DNA and live with greater purpose, compassion, and presence. In particular, Gene Key 37, called *Family Alchemy*, felt like a transmission into my family's journey, speaking directly to the transformations I had been living.

Through this Gene Key, I learned that the divine feminine was re-emerging via the sacred power of the mother—paradoxically, through the hearts of boys and men. This suggests that the imbalance of the feminine in our world didn't reside solely in women, but in how the feminine principle had been suppressed, especially within men. The rise of independence and sovereignty in women was not a departure from their feminine essence, but a counterbalance to restore wholeness.

This wisdom deeply echoed what I'd been witnessing in my own home. When boys are surrounded by love, supported emotionally, and allowed to remain connected to their innate sensitivity, they don't need to armor up against the world. They can grow into men who are whole, emotionally literate, and capable of co-creating a more balanced future. Raising two sons in tenderness and truth felt like sacred activism.

The 37th Siddhi, *Tenderness*, describes a new climate of care surrounding parents and children. In this future vision, feminine energy carries the blueprint of a more integrated society, and the masculine builds it into form—not through domination, but service. It's a radical reimagining of family, power, and what becomes possible when we soften the spaces between us.

I had moved countries, built an off-grid sanctuary, facilitated retreats, coached people through radical transformation, and given birth—twice, in the jungle, with no one present but my life partner, who stood by me not only as my beloved but as my birth doula. These are not just milestones. They are the lived moments of the shared path we had carved together through devotion, courage, and a deep commitment to inner and outer transformation.

Fabrice and I didn't just build homes—we built a life rooted in intention. Yes, he literally built our houses with his own hands, turning raw land into a place of refuge and regeneration, but there was more to it than that. Through all the uncertainty, the joy, the breakdowns, and the rebirths, we stayed present with the deeper work required not only to love one another but to grow alongside one another. This is what I've come to call *Relationshift,* the evolution of how we relate to ourselves, our partners, our communities, and the world around us. It is about choosing presence over patterns, which also means letting go of performative connection in favor of something more raw, real, and respectful.

For me as an individual, that looked like learning to speak my truth without guilt. For us as a couple, it looked like sitting in the fire together and choosing not to run. It meant Fabrice holding space for my unraveling—and me holding space for his. It meant remembering that healing doesn't happen alone, that it's okay to fall apart in each other's arms. Staying isn't about perfection; it's about commitment to becoming. It's not clean or linear. It's messy, sacred, and filled with paradox.

This journey—rooted in our bodies, shaped by parenthood, and mirrored in partnership— showed me that the deepest fulfillment didn't come from checking things off, but from becoming someone who lives with presence and integrity. Yes, we had lived out certain dreams that many dare only to name, but the real miracle was how we kept showing up together and for each other in truth and in love.

After twenty-five years of working on gender issues, I've come to realize that the core problem wasn't simply the social constructs of gender. It was the value we attached to those constructs—the worth assigned to being a boy or a girl, a man or a woman—and the power systems that reinforce them. Even in so-called progressive spaces, I've witnessed how women are often celebrated for adopting traits that mirror masculine ideals, while men who express tenderness or emotional depth are still seen as somehow "less than."

Generation after generation, we've been taught to distrust the feminine. This confusion has severed us from our true nature, dulling our connection to both the feminine and masculine energies that live within us all. Neither is superior; both are essential. Yet, we've come to equate surrender with weakness, softness with irrelevance, and intuition with irrationality.

This collective fear has roots in our ancestral memory—from times like the witch hunts, when women who carried healing knowledge, spiritual wisdom, or who simply lived outside patriarchal norms were persecuted, tortured, and silenced. The feminine was not just dismissed; it was hunted. That terror embedded itself in our bones, passed down as a quiet warning: don't stand out, don't speak up, and don't trust your own power.

I didn't expect to meet that fear so intimately in my own life. But that's exactly what happened when I lost my eyesight. There was nothing passive about the type of surrender that was asked of me. I could no longer navigate the world in the way I had always done. I had to learn to be led, to feel instead of see, and to open to uncertainty without collapsing. The process was active, soul-deep, and terrifying.

In my surrender, something ancient stirred—a knowing that power doesn't always look like control. Sometimes, it looks like letting go and listening, like trusting life to hold you when you can't hold yourself. From that bare, raw, disoriented space, I began to understand something else: we are not meant to do this alone. The path of remembering the feminine, of reclaiming our wholeness, asks for sisterhood.

Living in the jungle of Costa Rica taught me the true value of sisterhood, bringing me back to its essence and how it can be experienced daily. While I was slowly navigating the path toward healing my vision, I held space for a weekly women's circle, an interactive gathering for reflection and wisdom sharing. Preparing themes and prompts had always been part of my identity as a facilitator, but when I lost my eyesight, I felt as though I also lost that part of myself. How could I lead if I could no longer see?

This is where the medicine of sisterhood revealed itself. One by one, the women in the circle stepped forward to walk beside me. They read texts aloud, shared guided practices, and most importantly, reminded me how powerful we are in simply being there for each other. I didn't need to see to be seen. I didn't need to lead to hold space with love.

When women come together with full commitment, shared intention, and no judgment, something sacred happens. We help one another stay aligned, serving as mirrors for each other's truth. In that circle, I was heard and held in ways I had never experienced before. The support I received there was nothing short of communion.

At the end of one such gathering, I was given a pair of rainbow-colored wings that glowed in the dark. I clutched them tightly. For a year, I reflected on their meaning. Wings that gave off light in the darkness, providing a sense of possibility even when grounded. When I felt cut off from flow, as I had for the two years of my life that were suspended without sight, those wings reminded me that I was still in motion. I could still rise up.

I rediscovered the rare treasure of vulnerability and authenticity that arises when women sit together in a safe space. Though not all of us in the group knew each other, we trusted whoever had invited us and, by extension, extended that trust to one another. As we each shared our vulnerabilities, I felt truly held, safe to express my true feelings without pretending everything was fine. This safety felt nourishing and precious, and it allowed us to share deeply. We reflected on stories of motherhood, miscarriage, birth, death, fear, betrayal, loss, grief, and trauma.

Each woman's story resonated with another's, and our words weaved together into a shared feminine experience that we all related to. After sharing, we danced, each song taking us deeper into ourselves and into connection with one another. We danced our prayers, desires, wishes, new beginnings, and closures, feeling so close to each other as we did. That is the beauty of the circle.

As I danced, I felt and embraced my heart, connecting with all parts of myself. Projections and reflections of myself danced alongside me, beautifully intertwined in a collective experience. All around me were whispers of, "Me too. I feel this way too. I think this way too."

Sisterhood offers a sanctuary of empathy, understanding, and unconditional support, where women can share their experiences, challenges, and triumphs without judgment. These sacred circles offer reflections of our own struggles and strengths, fostering a sense of belonging and solidarity when we otherwise might feel alone. This support not only nurtures personal growth but also strengthens the fabric of our communities, offering transformative healing on an individual and collective level.

As we uplift and empower each other, we heal old wounds, break cycles of self-betrayal, and create a ripple effect of positive change. The power of sisterhood lies in its ability to remind us that we are not alone and that, together, we can overcome any adversity and thrive. Through the shared healing it brings, we can cultivate resilience, compassion, and a deeper connection to our authentic selves and each other.

Once again, this all comes down to surrender and

the willingness to let go of who we think we need to be so that we can become who we truly are. As sisterhood shows us, this need not be a solitary act. It can be witnessed, welcomed, and echoed back with love. When that is done, healing is not only possible—it is inevitable.

Allowing myself to be held both as a woman and as a leader was a challenge for me. But vulnerability is both possible and necessary, and losing my eyesight taught me the value of interdependence. Life is inherently interdependent, yet we often adopt the belief that we must be entirely independent, as if needing others makes us weak.

Like it convinces so many of us, society taught me that to be strong and successful, I had to rely solely on myself. And, as a woman, the pressure to prove my strength and capability was only exacerbated. From an early age, I internalized the belief that needing help was dangerous, even shameful. There was no room for softness or uncertainty. So I constructed an identity around independence, convinced that showing need would be mistaken for weakness. I wore my self-sufficiency like armor, even when it was quietly cutting me off from connection, tenderness, and truth.

Developmental psychology and trauma studies have long shown that when our basic needs for connection and consistent caregiving aren't met in childhood, we adapt. We learn that vulnerability is unsafe and needing is risky. As children, we internalize the message: no one is coming; I have to do this myself. And so, independence becomes our shield—our way of staying in control in a world that has felt unpredictable or unreliable.

Experts like Bessel van der Kolk, who wrote *The Body Keeps the Score*, describe how these early adaptations become embedded in the physical self. Our nervous systems learn to stay alert, braced, and self-contained. Attachment theory echoes this, explaining how children who grow up without secure bonds often develop avoidant strategies, choosing distance over closeness and self-sufficiency over the risk of disappointment.

Pete Walker calls this "hyper-independence" in adults with complex PTSD, an intelligent but limiting strategy meant to protect the heart. Dr. Stephen Porges' Polyvagal Theory speaks to how trauma reshapes our biology, pushing us into survival states of hyperarousal or collapse. I had spent most of my life in that subtle but persistent state of hyperarousal—always "on," always prepared, always doing.

Sure, it *looked* like strength—and in many ways, it was. But beneath it was something else: a deep, unspoken belief that I couldn't depend on anyone and that needing others would only lead to disappointment or pain. Like many women, I learned early on that if my emotional or physical needs weren't consistently met, I had to meet them myself. And for a while, that method worked. I became a resourceful, capable, and fiercely self-reliant woman.

In my professional life, I felt the need to constantly prove my competence. Admitting that I needed help or support seemed like admitting failure. So, I built a wall around my vulnerabilities, convincing myself that I could and should handle everything on my own. Hiding became a survival strategy, a way to protect myself from judgment, rejection, and the fear of being perceived as weak.

Over the years, I came to understand that my fierce independence wasn't simply a personality trait—it was a trauma response. When our basic needs for connection and support are unmet, especially in our formative years, we develop coping mechanisms based on this knowledge. Hoping to protect ourselves from disappointment, rejection, or further trauma, we tell ourselves it is too risky to rely on others. As a result, we become self-sufficient to a fault, often isolating ourselves emotionally and rejecting offers of help even when we desperately need them. So we learn to take care of and comfort ourselves, telling ourselves it doesn't matter—we don't need them anyway. The confusion seeps in when we need help but are convinced we don't want it. Perhaps we don't even know how to ask for it or aren't willing to accept it when it is offered.

This trauma response can then carry over into adulthood, manifesting as a staunch clinging to our sense of independence. This shaped the way I mothered, the way I led, and the way I suffered (silently, and often unnecessarily). I told myself I was strong enough to handle it all. I didn't ask for help, even when I longed for it. I judged myself for needing it. I pushed through, even when my body was begging me to rest. I only accepted an alternative way of being when I was left with no other choice.

I now understand how harsh this belief system was for my body and soul. Humans are inherently social beings who thrive on connection and belonging. Sometimes, we are able to face challenges all on our own, and sometimes we must ask for and accept help. Both realities are okay. The key is to recognize our needs without judgment, and to understand that interdependence is a natural and necessary part of being human.

It took losing my eyesight for my carefully constructed independence to unravel. Suddenly, independence wasn't an option. I couldn't muscle through or perform my way out. I had to rely on others for the most basic tasks. All the protective narratives I had built around strength and capability dissipated. Only then did I see these problematic tendencies for what they were. It wasn't just my eyes that had failed me—it was the illusion of safety through separation.

Losing my vision was the initiation I didn't know I needed. Ultimately, what I found in the darkness was not weakness, but a lesson in trusting and receiving. I learned that being held wouldn't lead to abandonment or betrayal. The trauma that once taught me not to need anyone was now asking to be unlearned, encouraging me to be seen in my unguarded moments, and showing me I would be loved anyway.

I had built myself, my career, and my sense of self on being a fully independent and strong woman who didn't need anyone, least of all a man. Abandoning the identity I had built around self-reliance was humbling, even disorienting. But it also forced me to confront something deeper: the fears I had carried for so long. Through this process, I learned that true strength came from embracing vulnerability, not hiding from it. Accepting help did not diminish my worth or capabilities; instead, it enriched my life and relationships. True independence is a myth. We all need each other.

The dark night of my ego had revealed how much and for how long I had relied on the façade of independence. Those superficial personas had names: *I've got this. I don't need help. I'm fine.* They looked like over-functioning, like always being the one who holds it all together, like showing up with a smile even when I was falling apart inside. I wore them so well that I almost believed them myself. But they were costumes stitched from fear—the fear that if I revealed my need, I would be seen as weak, unworthy, or too much.

My soul invited me to shed these false appearances and embrace the rawness of my true needs. Without my sight, I needed help—daily, intimately, and humbly. And what I discovered through that necessity was the quiet, undeniable strength of interdependence. Not dependency born from helplessness, but connection born from truth.

When my sisters read aloud for me, when my children learned to meet me with tenderness, when my partner showed up without needing me to be strong, I no longer felt diminished. Instead, I felt human. I felt loved and powerful in a way I never had when I was holding everything alone. I felt like myself.

As we navigate our unique journeys, it's crucial to surround ourselves with empathetic, supportive individuals who respect our boundaries and honor our process, wherever we are at. This support network can help us relearn trust and redefine independence in a healthier, more balanced way. Our power lies not in isolation but in the courage to connect, to need and be needed.

Women often hide their needs out of the fear of being a burden. As we struggle to maintain an illusion of control, we often find ourselves succumbing to isolation and burnout. This hiding is not our personal choice; it is a reflection of broader societal expectations placed on us. Women are often socialized to be caregivers, to prioritize others' needs over their own, and to bear their burdens silently. This cultural narrative discourages women from showing vulnerability or asking for help, perpetuating the perceived virtue of independence and self-reliance.

In workplaces dominated by patriarchal norms, showing vulnerability can be particularly risky, as it might be seen as a lack of professionalism or competence. This fear drives us to present a polished exterior, even when we are struggling internally. But when we allow ourselves to be seen, when we ask for and accept help, we break the cycle of isolation. And, from there, we create spaces where others feel safe to do the same, fostering a culture of mutual support and understanding.

In embracing my own capacity for interdependence, I discovered the strength in community and connection. I found peace in knowing that needing others is not a weakness but a fundamental aspect of being human. By sharing our struggles and supporting each other, we build resilience and solidarity. This shift from hiding to openness transforms our relationships and empowers us to live more authentically.

As women, we can challenge the societal norms that pressure us to hide. We can redefine strength to include vulnerability and interdependence. By doing so, we not only heal ourselves but also create a more compassionate and supportive environment for everyone. It is through this collective effort that we can truly thrive, embracing our full selves without fear or shame.

"I wish I could show you
when you are lonely or in
darkness the astonishing
light of your being."

~ Hafiz

chapter seven

CALLING BACK THE SOUL

I had spent years gathering titles, roles, and experiences that shaped how the world saw me and how I saw myself. Then, in the stillness that followed my unraveling, none of them seemed to hold meaning anymore. The achievements, the causes, the credentials—they had formed a shell around something I hadn't yet dared to fully meet. There was something inside of me that was yearning to be known, an invisible intelligence I couldn't quite identify. It was a pulse beneath the noise, and I longed to strip everything else away so I could touch something real and whole.

In my search for healing, I found myself delving deeper, seeking to know myself beyond the accumulated identities on my résumé. I sought to eliminate the polarities, wanting to reach a place of oneness, but all

I could feel was a numb sense of nothingness. I didn't find the peace I had imagined. Instead, there was just a vast, quiet space where nothing was mirrored back to me—no pain, no clarity, no answers.

So, as I had done before, I tried to listen differently. I stayed with it, allowing myself to be with what was left behind when everything else fell away. With all of my "accomplishing" gone, I shifted my focus away from what other people thought of me and into inner space to listen to something deeper. In the darkness, I detected a quiet awareness. It wasn't a vision in the traditional sense, but more like a flicker of felt memory. There was a presence within me that was beyond language, an internal light that lives in all of us, even when we forget it is there.

What I saw was that we were not separate beings struggling alone in the dark but particles of light, scattered across the universe like star seeds, each of us a fragment of something ancient and whole. In the vision, those fragments converged, weaving themselves into one great luminous body: the Sun. Its pure, radiant consciousness sent us forth to another vast surface, the Earth. And here, in these fragile human forms, we landed.

The vision didn't come with instructions or meaning neatly spelled out, and I couldn't fully make sense of it at the time. But the image stayed with me, burned into my heart in a way that didn't need to be understood to be true. It sustained me in moments when everything else fell apart. It reminded me, quietly and insistently, that we were all light on the inside.

That inner light kept calling me, whispering through all of the numbness and forgetting. It was asking me to remember, but at that point, I couldn't truly listen. I didn't yet know how to answer. The silence between us—the light within and the self I had become—was wide. But something in me was beginning to turn toward it.

The words of one of my favorite songs, "Blessed We Are" by Peia, spoke directly to the part of me that was trying to wake up. I would listen to that song on repeat, letting it wash over me like medicine. It became a lifeline when my own voice had gone quiet, a reminder that even when I felt numb and disconnected, there was still something holy unfolding through the pain.

What was my calling? I couldn't identify it anymore, but I was aching to know it. I simply needed to remember who I had been before I took on so many layers. I needed to remember that this life, even in its most painful moments, was sacred. I would often cry as I listened to that song. I knew I was blessed and that we were sacred, but what was my true calling, my true passion? I cried because I couldn't remember.

As I did, I felt not just my own pain but the pain of my people. This is probably how all Palestinians feel—to have a sense of something that they don't necessarily remember or believe. We are a people with a deep sense of history and connection to our land, yet the constant struggle and displacement have left us in a state of collective amnesia. We ache to remember our true essence, our true calling.

I was born in a country where three different religions hold the meaning of "truth"—not *the* truth, but *their* truth. Every "truth" offers us guidance for a way of living, behaving, treating one another, and taking care of the earth and its plants and animals. Yet each religion has gotten a bit lost, trying to tell others how they should live, relate, behave, and believe. Focused on imposing a viewpoint, each tradition has lost sight of the original intention, confusing the message with the messenger and the destination with the intention. And here we are—here I am—trying to make sense of it all.

Not seeing was the ultimate survival strategy for my family, a behavior deeply reinforced by our culture and history. Growing up in a war-torn area riddled with thousands of years of conflict and intergenerational trauma, the act of "not seeing" became a means of enduring the harsh realities surrounding us.

In my personal experience, not seeing took on more than just metaphorical significance, even in childhood. It adapted to a literal and psychological form that helped me survive as a Palestinian in Israel. The complexities of my identity, the friction of differing cultural and religious norms, and the constant undercurrent of political tension created an environment where ignorance was not only bliss but a necessary shield. By not fully seeing or acknowledging the full extent of the undeniable conflict and disparities, I could navigate my daily life without being constantly overwhelmed by the weight of historical and current injustices.

This survival strategy extended beyond my own personal coping mechanisms. It was woven into the very fabric of my family's way of life. My parents, grandparents, and ancestors had all learned, in various ways, to shield their eyes from the full brutality of their reality to protect their mental and emotional well-being. This cultural practice of selective sight allowed us to focus on immediate needs and joys, to find moments of peace amidst chaos, and to carry on despite the seemingly endless cycle of trauma and unrest.

Attending a Jesuit school as a Palestinian added layers to this complex strategy. There, I was exposed to a different worldview, a set of values and beliefs that often clashed with my own. In this environment, not seeing became a tool for integration and coexistence. It allowed me to engage with diverse perspectives while maintaining a sense of inner peace and identity. It was not about denial but about selective focus—choosing what to see and what to let pass by, like filtering the air I breathed.

Later in life, as I reflected on my journey and my writing, I came to understand that "not seeing" also prevented me from fully understanding my own purpose and potential. It shielded me from pain but also from deep self-awareness and growth. When I looked deeper, I saw that there was a perpetual darkness hovering over the heads of the Palestinian people, a shadow of forgotten dreams and suppressed hopes born from years of conflict, loss, and the constant fight for identity. We were caught between the yearning for peace and the relentless reality of our struggles. In that darkness, it was easy to lose sight of the light within us.

Writing this book, I had to commit to seeing clearly, to understanding my experiences without the filter of fear or avoidance. I had to invite the dark parts to come forward, knowing that the darkness was not the enemy but the teacher. I had learned from my loss of vision how darkness could show us the depths of our resilience and the strength of our spirit, reminding us that, even in the absence of clear direction, there is a sacredness to our existence. By acknowledging and accepting this darkness, we can honor the full spectrum of our humanity.

In the same vein, the sorrow, anger, and fear that we encounter along the way are all part of this journey. To truly understand my own calling, I felt I had to embrace the collective pain, the feeling of being blessed yet burdened. It was a heavy weight, but it seemed like the only way to get closer to who I was and where I came from.

I realized that letting go of my need to accomplish and focusing inward allowed me to listen to the whispers of my inner light. This journey wasn't about erasing the darkness but about acknowledging it and understanding that within it is a connection to the light we all carry. Through this, I felt I would learn to remember who I truly was and to trust the sacredness of this life. And so, I continued to listen to the song, to the cries of my heart and the hearts of my people, knowing that in our collective darkness, the seeds of light were waiting to be remembered and reborn.

Once I regained my sight, I had assumed clarity would follow, sharpening my vision for the future into something certain and defined. But sight doesn't always mean clarity, and clarity doesn't always arrive all at once. For a while, everything remained blurry—not just externally but within. I had felt an immediate pull to return to the "normal path"—but what is normal anyway? Everyone's definition varies depending on our experiences, backgrounds, and interpretations of reality.

My definition of normal was based on the familiar rhythms of my career as an international consultant, engaging with institutions, traveling to conflict zones, and advising on policy and gender equity. That was the work I knew how to do and that had once defined me. There was comfort in the structure I once had, and there was clarity in being useful, contributing to something larger than myself.

But something had changed, and it was not just the setting (though I did now live higher in the mountains with a beautiful view of the rolling green hills and the sky, which I could finally see). I also had an internet connection at home, allowing me to work remotely. There was no need to go anywhere anymore. I could create my entire life from my creative sanctuary and serve my function as an international consultant for countries in conflict while living in this idyllic environment. I could fight for women's rights and against gender-based violence, all while celebrating feminine energy and Mother Earth in the jungle.

My body was in motion, saying yes to assignments and invitations, yet my soul was no longer simply following; it was watching. It was present in a way I couldn't quite name but that I could feel in everything. Meetings that used to excite me now felt hollow. Deadlines came and went, but I moved through them differently—slower, more porous, less armored.

I remember sitting in a high-level meeting in Geneva, surrounded by brilliant minds and urgent agendas. On paper, it was a moment of success. But internally, I felt like a visitor from another world. The conversation was sharp and strategic, but something essential was missing. I was no longer there to fix. I was listening for something deeper, something the spreadsheets and policies didn't address. I wanted to get at the soul of the work—the soul of the people.

I realized I couldn't go back to the version of me that once wore that identity like a well-fitted coat. That version had already served its purpose. Now, I needed to integrate this new awareness. I needed to walk the old path differently. The pandemic had changed the world, creating an expectation for things to be different, yet outwardly, life remained unchanged. Inwardly, though, everything felt different. In the same way, after my own transformative experience, I felt closer to myself. I was grateful for the vision I once had and content with where I was, yet a burning passion to serve still smoldered within me. The indefinable desire for something more was still there, and I ached with it. This kind of ache is what pushes us humans to transcend our perceived limitations and achieve greatness.

Sometimes, I can't stand the paradox of my life, with all of its complexities and uncertainties. Why did there always seem to be a desire for more deep inside of me? Why the yearning to have more, do more, be more? Why wasn't it enough? It was a question that beckoned me to look within and confront the parts of myself that yearned for more, constantly striving for something beyond my current state.

This burning desire I couldn't even name felt like another core belief that needed unpacking. The belief of "enoughness" was a beautiful place to return to, embracing all the seemingly paradoxical parts of humanness that a tidy, efficient worldview often rejected. Yet the concept challenged me deeply.

There are parts of us that don't fit neatly into professional boxes or productivity metrics, like the part of me that can hold space for others' grief with grace—and then collapse in tears afterward without knowing why. Or the part that can speak on global stages with clarity and conviction yet still doubts her worth when alone. Or the part that longs to serve the world and, in the same breath, dreams of disappearing into silence and being accountable to no one.

There's also the part that wants to believe in transformation but is also heartbroken to see how little changes on the surface. And the part that yearns for community but often feels safest alone. And the part that trusts the divine and still fears being abandoned. These are the parts that a results-driven, hyper-rational world doesn't know what to do with. They are too fluid and feeling, too slow and nonlinear. They are too much.

I've come to see all of these parts not as weaknesses but as signs of being deeply human and deeply alive. They are the parts that know how to sit with mystery, how to hold joy and pain in the same breath, how to listen for what is emerging rather than forcing what has been simply because it is what we already know. They are the ones that teach me how to lead in spite of the fears and doubts that inevitably arise.

So I began to walk differently—not away from the world I once inhabited but through it, with new eyes and a softened heart. I still took on consulting work and joined rooms of strategy and negotiation, but I no longer left myself at the door when I did. I started asking different questions—not just about impact and indicators but about *integrity, resonance,* and *alignment.*

Instead of jumping straight into action plans, I would begin meetings with a pause, a grounding breath, a moment of presence. It felt small, even awkward at first—but I noticed how it changed the field. People settled as something unseen opened up among us all. I started listening not only to what was being said but to what was left unspoken: the grief underneath the policies, the exhaustion behind the performance, the longing for something more human and more real.

As I allowed myself to bring the unseen into the room, I spoke not just from the expert in me but from the part that had walked through darkness and come out with a different kind of knowing. I didn't have to prove anything anymore. I just had to be there, fully. That was the shift: not doing more, but being more.

Perhaps this was what my soul had been asking of me all along—not to abandon the work, but to allow these contradictions to live at the center of it. To let the light and the dark sit side by side, no longer hiding the soft, intuitive, mystical parts of me in order to appear credible or efficient. Because the deeper I go, the more I realize: wholeness is never tidy. It is textured, complicated, and beautifully unresolved.

I've come to love naming these paradoxes—not to solve or fix them but to see them, giving them air and space and dignity. It's one of my favorite practices to offer my clients when they feel overwhelmed by the noise within. We sit together and begin to name the parts with curiosity rather than judgment. We don't have to love each one, but we can ask ourselves to respect any parts that feel real and resonant because, if they're alive within us, they have something to teach.

These are some of the paradoxical parts that often arise—maybe you'll recognize a few of your own:

The part that wants to lead, and the part that longs to hide.

The part that believes in justice, and the part that's exhausted by fighting.

The part that craves deep intimacy, and the part terrified of being truly seen.

The part that wants to be wildly free, and the part that yearns for safety and structure.

The part that's filled with compassion for others, and the part that judges them silently.

The part that dreams big, and the part that whispers, "You'll never make it."

The part that's deeply spiritual, and the part that rolls its eyes at ritual.

The part that is clear and visionary, and the part that still doesn't know what she wants.

Each of these holds both wisdom and tension, which, together, form the mosaic of our humanity. The more I sit with these parts—mine and others'—the more I see that the goal is not to eliminate the contradictions, but to build a home spacious enough to hold them all. After all, life isn't about fitting into a neat box; it's about acknowledging and respecting the chaotic and contradictory elements that make us whole.

As I reflect on these experiences, I realize that the path of my career may appear unchanged, but my approach to it is fundamentally transformed. My passion to serve is no longer about checking off achievements, but about embracing and nurturing the undefinable, burning desire within. This ache for more isn't a dissatisfaction; it's the human drive to reach beyond the ordinary and touch the extraordinary.

Most people's predominant regret on their deathbed is, "I wish I had had the courage to listen to the voice inside instead of letting other people dictate the direction of my life. I wish I had had the courage to do what I knew I came here to do." This quote is paraphrased from the work of Bronnie Ware, an Australian nurse who worked in palliative care. In her book, *The Top Five Regrets of the Dying*, she shares insights from her experiences with patients at the end of their lives. She identified the persistence of wishing we had had the courage to live a life true to ourselves, rather than that which others had expected of us.

I rarely listened to what others told me about my path and followed my heart every step of the way, yet still I found myself unsure of my soul's true purpose. I was still exploring, still searching for that deeper understanding. Or was I already living it?

Some people know exactly what their calling is and where to focus. From the outside, this may look like a straight line, an inner candle flame that never flickers. But what about those of us who never got this feeling of urgent need? Or who just ignored it, pushing it to the side? "Listen to your heart," people often say, to which I would respond, "I *am* listening!" But my soul's passion? My lifelong dream? That kind of desire seemed ever-shifting, evolving along with the soul itself. Sometimes it felt like I wanted to embrace more of life than what life in the flesh allowed for.

There is a distinction between who we are and who we can become. The invitation to lose sight of the ego is often a call to stop identifying through its narrow lens. This desire for self-discovery is what brought me to this leg of the journey.

I didn't know it at the time, but my return to Israel and Palestine in April 2023 marked a turning point. I was reconnecting with my destiny—or at least brushing against it. What unfolded wasn't planned but emerged through presence, movement, and deep listening. I found myself moving alone between worlds. Between checkpoints and realities, conversations that carried centuries of sorrow, and quiet moments that felt like threads of hope. I reunited with two dear friends, and each encounter was intimate and necessary, as though we were remembering soul contracts long buried beneath the weight of history.

I also moved between physical realms: Bethlehem

and Kfar Tavor, Jaffa and Haifa, Ramallah and Jerusalem. The lines between "here," "there," "us," and "them" began to lose meaning. I crossed borders with growing awareness—not just of the stark contradictions on either side but of something rising within me. I began to feel the contours of a new vision forming. It wasn't a grand solution or a perfect roadmap, but it did seem to be a deeper connection to what truly mattered. I was moving through the spaces between conflict, guided by something ancient and quiet that asked to be witnessed. That's when I began to see not through my physical eyes but through the depths of my soul. In the process of reconnecting with my purpose, I had to peel away everything I thought defined me. Titles, roles, and even the impact I had been so proud of all had to fall away so I could hear something quieter and truer.

One of the practices that helped me was coming back to my body, especially the solar plexus, which holds the fire of identity and will. It speaks not in language, but in instinct and resonance. So, I began placing my hand just below my ribcage and listening for that deep, pulsing knowing inside of me. And I invite you, too—readers, clients, and companions on this journey—to try this for yourself. Take a breath. Then, place your hand on your solar plexus and ask: "Who am I when I am not performing? What is calling me?"

For me, the answer was clear. What I had to do was give voice to what lives in the unseen layers of experience. I had to share because I couldn't not share. I had to write. I didn't do it for approval, but because my soul sought the expansion and the connection to its infinite nature. I had to tear down whatever obstacles might try to confine or dilute that truth.

I now see how little my calling has to do with the words and titles on my résumé and how much it has to do with how I feel when I'm fully alive. My soul has a theme song that sings of freedom and peace, and its writing is about expression and expansion. That's what I want for you too: not a purpose that fits a mold, but a purpose that sets something inside of you on fire.

At the beginning of this book, I shared a quote from Rumi: "Out beyond ideas of wrongdoing and rightdoing, there is a field. I will meet you there." This quote beautifully encapsulates a critical realization I've had: My journey is just a mirror of where I am standing. My self-responsibility is my destination, and it has nothing to do with anyone else. None of my experiences or challenges are about other people; they are only about me.

I believe that I lost my vision so that I could discover within myself where I had already lost my vision for my destiny. I had to lose my vision to find where, why, and what I am choosing to live. In the end, all of the contradictions are true. I live the life of an international consultant, traveling around conflict zones, training people on the ground and in institutions, and working with people in and out of crisis. I also have a life in the jungle of Costa Rica, closer to the earth and the pace of nature, moving with the rise and fall of the sun and the rain, fluctuating with the rhythms of childbirth and childcare. Here, I feel a clearer understanding of the interdependence of life on earth and the natural interplay of human dynamics. I witness conflicts within myself that are just as strong as those outside of myself. I have discovered a deeper understanding of the human (soul) level of living a life of balance.

I've come to understand that living in balance isn't about perfection or getting things "right." It's about honoring the human experience while remaining connected to the soul's deeper knowing. On the soul level, there is no judgment—no right or wrong—only experiences that guide us back to remembering who we are. This shift in perspective allowed me to hold both my pain and my joy without labeling them as failures or successes. I began to see that all moments, even those that are messy and uncertain, carry an invitation to return to balance between doing and being, striving and surrendering.

In a world that is so often divided by dichotomies, consider this: There is no right and wrong. We are given a life on Earth to explore and experience different situations in which we get to sense what is good for us and what feels right. Sometimes, we get lost in judgment of our own experience as well as those of others. Beneath the judgments, there is insecurity. Beneath the insecurity, there is a lack of self-love and self-awareness.

We project upon others what we think we should or shouldn't do. If we can remember that there is only the experience, no right or wrong, we can find peace.

Feel into that field that exists beyond the right, wrong, good, and bad. I always thought I was there. I thought of myself as tolerant, but losing my eyesight brought me deeper insights into the judgments I still had about myself and others, about different situations and the environment I was born into.

I had to wait in the womb until my mum was ready to give birth to me. The story goes, according to her, that I was so ready to be born that her water broke as soon as she arrived at the hospital, and I nearly fell on the floor while the nurses were arguing over who was going to catch me. In a way, this birth story is a reflection of my life. There is a pattern in my life where I have ideas and feel ready to release them in the impulsive energy of the moment. I am ready to fly, yet I am always waiting for someone, something to give me the okay, to catch me if I fall.

These past years have brought this to an extreme, as I have waited for my eyesight to come back, like in the play *Waiting for Godot*, or the waiting room in *Oh! The Places You'll Go* by Dr. Seuss, which I used to read to my kids when they were younger. I have felt stuck in this waiting room all my life, waiting for my life to begin, and now I feel finally ready.

The savior I have been waiting for all along is me. It sounds cliché, but it is true. On this journey of soul discovery—*sole* discovery—we are the ones we have been waiting for. This is it. My heart's true desire is like a living dream, constantly evolving with each breath, each prayer, embracing all the hats I wear and all the roles I play. My heart's path has led me to become a mother and guided me to empower women, embrace a feminine vision with a masculine focus, and dance with my soul, ultimately connecting to my spirit. In the end, perhaps it's about finding peace within the paradox, accepting that life's complexity is part of its beauty. The journey is ongoing, and with each step, I'm learning to balance my external achievements with inner fulfillment, navigating the new normal, one breath at a time.

I've stopped needing the answers to be clean. I no longer chase the illusion of a fixed identity or a final destination. My soul did not come here to be efficient—it came here to *remember*. To express. To feel. To connect. To dissolve the walls between worlds, between selves, between what is and what could be.

If I had to say what I'm here for, it would be this:

To bring light into the forgotten places. To midwife stories that heal and reveal. To hold space for paradox. To love with both tenderness and truth. To walk between the worlds and remind us that we belong to each other. To activate peace—from the inside out.

This isn't a mission I fulfill; it's a frequency I return to again and again—especially when I forget. So, if you're here reading this, you, too, are being called to remember who you already are beneath the noise. Listen, let go, and follow that quiet, relentless voice inside that says: *This is why you came.*

"Our work is to make ourselves visible in the world. This is the soul's journey, and the soul would much rather fail at its own life than succeed at someone else's."

~ David Whyte

chapter eight

VISION BEYOND SIGHT

Not long after I began to see again, I stood barefoot in the early morning light, the world around me soft with dew and silence. Something in the air felt different—clearer, as though I was being shown life for the very first time again. In that moment, that prior vision returned. Each of us as a particle of light, and when our outer shells begin to crumble—through illness, loss, or change—we fall to earth, not as something broken, but as something becoming. I had seen this before, in the depths of darkness, and the message was always the same: the light is not something to seek. It lives within us, waiting to be remembered. Even in the heaviest hours, it flickers and guides us.

In traditional Palestinian oral history, memory is an act of resistance. In the absence of written acknowledgment, memory is what keeps history alive. My loss of vision had forced me to rely on memory rather than sight. In the early months of my blindness, I clung to it as a means of orientation. I traced the shapes of my children's faces in my mind, recalling the exact curve of their smiles and the way their eyes sparkled in the sun. I walked through my home using memory, counting steps, feeling textures, piecing together the space not by seeing but by remembering.

This practice of remembering became more than just a survival mechanism—it became a healing mechanism. It made me recognize the stories my people carried in their hearts, the ones that have been passed down not through ink and paper but through whisper, song, and the careful retelling of what was and what was lost. I began to understand that what we remember—how we tell our stories—becomes just as powerful as what is written.

Healing, I realized, was about not only the restoration of sight but the restoration of memory. It was about holding onto truth even when the world insists it does not exist. When I could not see, I learned to listen. I listened to the voices of my ancestors in the stories my mother told me, in the verses of poetry recited at family gatherings, in the hymns of longing that echoed through our traditions.

The world often only acknowledges what is visible, what is recorded, what is convenient to remember. But what happens when an entire people's story is erased, rewritten, or ignored? Memory is how we ensure that what has been denied is still held, honored, and spoken into existence. In that sense, it is a bridge between erasure and existence.

For decades, Palestinians have lived in a reality where their past is denied, their land renamed, and their history reframed. Borders, maps, and narratives have been altered to shape a version of history that serves power. As a Palestinian, I have spent my life navigating a space where my people's truth is a whispered resistance rather than a recognized reality.

Losing my sight made me understand, on a visceral level, what it means to be unseen—not just as an individual but as a people. It made me confront what it means to be erased, to exist only in the margins of someone else's story. When the world does not acknowledge your pain, when it rewrites your past and dictates your future, you begin to wonder how much of your existence is your own.

I recall moments in my childhood when history lessons omitted our presence. The maps in our textbooks did not show the Palestine my grandparents had spoken of. The villages they described were ghost towns on the pages of official narratives, erased from documentation but alive in their memories. I remember the first time I truly understood this gap—that what I was taught in school did not align with what my family carried in their hearts.

For a long time, I tried to reconcile these

contradictions. I wanted to believe that if I studied enough, if I excelled at the language of the system, I could find a way to bridge these realities. But the deeper I delved, the more I saw how certain forms of erasure were intentional, how it is power that dictates what is seen and unseen. And when you are not seen, you are vulnerable to being misunderstood, misrepresented, or forgotten.

Losing my sight made this metaphor literal. Suddenly, I found myself in a world where people assumed what I needed, what I felt, and what I could or could not do—often without ever asking me. The loss of vision forced me into the shadows of perception, where assumptions replaced truth, where the absence of sight became an absence of identity in the eyes of others.

But if being unseen is a form of erasure, then reclaiming our stories—our truths—is an act of defiance. I had been living outside of Israel for thirty years, exploring various conflict zones, searching for answers, and discovering more questions along the way. I believed that if I worked in conflict zones that were not "mine," they would not trigger me. I thought I would not become emotionally involved and could remain neutral. How foolish.

Every conflict engages our emotions on some level, regardless of whether it is ours or someone else's. Conflict lies at the core of human relations, but conflict itself holds no moral charge. It is natural, necessary, and neutral. Our human experience, however, is never neutral. Conflict touches our emotions, values, and histories. True neutrality, then, is not about disengagement or indifference; it is the inner capacity to stay grounded amidst intensity. From this place of centered presence, we gain the freedom to respond with clarity rather than react from wounding. Neutrality is the gateway to freedom.

When I visited my homeland in April 2023, I found myself laughing as I walked from the plane through the tunnel that led to the airport. It was not laughter born out of amusement but, rather, a release of pent-up emotions. Propaganda adorned the walls of the tunnel, highlights from Israel's role in saving Jews from all corners of the world. Totally absent was any mention of the local population of Palestinians that I belonged to, the people of the same land who had paid such a high price for the realization of this celebrated dream state.

Israel had disregarded the existence of this other nation, whose culture, language, and narrative were hidden from public discourse. And yet Israel's own narrative was crumbling under the weight of its internal struggles, the illusion of democracy fading away.

What struck me as I laughed was the fact that I was no longer triggered as I witnessed this political scene that was devoid of true democratic values. For three decades, during every visit to my family in Jaffa, I would drown in tension and a sense of injustice. The anger of the oppressed would well up inside me, and I found it difficult to interact with the outside world. To cope, I would detach myself, seeking solace in the comfort of the beach and the warmth of family.

But this time, something had changed. I felt the joy of equanimity and the magic of remaining unaffected by the chaos and violence that surrounded me. It was not that the situation had improved. In fact, it had worsened; the crisis had reached a tipping point. Yet I found myself undisturbed by it. I hadn't become insensitive, but I had become acutely aware of my environment and learned to deal with my emotional triggers. The teachings of spiritual psychology and my healing journey were bearing fruit. I could finally see beyond the surface.

Once I regained my eyesight and saw the world again, I saw it differently. The experience of blindness had stripped away illusion, forcing me to confront truths I had ignored. It made me question not just what I was seeing but how I was seeing.

Before, I had taken sight for granted, assuming that what was in front of me was the full story. But blindness had shown me that vision was not just physical— it was perceptual. What we choose to see and acknowledge is what defines our reality.

In regaining sight, I also reclaimed my right to see, to remember, and to name my own experience. I learned that healing was not just about recovering physical vision—it was about reclaiming the power of perception. I saw how the world constructs narratives, deciding which truths to illuminate and which to keep in darkness. And I realized that true vision is the ability to see beyond these constructions, to recognize the unseen and hold space for the stories that history tries to erase.

Healing became an act of redefining reality—not just my own but the collective reality of my people. If blindness had been a metaphor for erasure, then reclaiming sight was a declaration that I—we—still exist in spite of the margins we have been placed in.

Reclaiming sight also meant recognizing that I had been raised in an environment defined by a *Drama Triangle*, a psychological and social model of human interaction wherein not only individuals and families but even entire religions cycle through the roles of victim, persecutor, and savior. I could see it in my own home, where blame, guilt, and rescue were constant, and I could see it reflected in the way Judaism, Christianity, and Islam each claimed these roles at different times in history, seeing themselves as the persecuted, justifying acts of power as the persecutor, or stepping in as the savior of humanity. According to this model, every conflict—whether personal, familial, or political—plays out through three deeply ingrained roles:

The Victim: The one who suffers, feels powerless, waits for rescue or justice.

The Perpetrator: The one who inflicts harm, knowingly or unknowingly, often repeating patterns of their own unhealed pain.

The Rescuer: The one who intervenes, believing they can "fix" the situation, protect the victim, or restore balance.

Each role feeds the other, the victim reinforcing the perpetrator's justification for control and the rescuer, despite their good intentions, enabling dependency and preventing true empowerment. In turn, the perpetrator, feeling threatened, only intensifies their grip. And so the cycle continues.

The Drama Triangle dynamic was developed by psychologist Stephen Karpman. It is a cycle that keeps individuals, communities, and even whole societies trapped in narratives of pain, blame, and dependence. In this dynamic, there is no space for any vision other than the one proclaimed by whoever holds power—who wins the war, who controls the resources to sustain the war or occupation, and who manipulates the story to their advantage.

In such a dynamic, where power and control dominate, it becomes clear that, ultimately, all of us, regardless of who and what we are, are seeking approval and love on a visceral level. As Michael Brown wrote in *The Presence Process*, "All behaviors we witnessed during our interaction with others that aren't acts of unconditional love are unconscious pleas for unconditional love." It is as if love were taken away from us, just like we were taken away from our mothers, separated from her at the hour of our birth.

Love is inherent to our way of being. That's where

the waiting comes in—waiting to understand that love is all there is and that it is inherent to our humanity. Love is the act of the creator, whatever it is we prefer to call it. There is no need to do anything or go anywhere to feel love or be loved. Whatever shape or form we have, love is our nature. Without it, we wouldn't even be here.

It is written in so many different ways and across all platforms, in commercials, books, and public spaces. Yet the obvious gets lost exactly because it is so obvious, and then we minimize it. It isn't that simple, we think. It *can't* be that simple. Yet, after living in the dark for two years, I know, deep inside, that love is all there is for me. And that's the point: It's for me to understand, not for me to impose. It's not for me to teach or do anything at all with, other than feel the certainty of it within me.

Right before I lost my eyesight, I sent out a news-letter about my vision for 2020. First and foremost, I saw peace in the Middle East happening that year. That was my vision. Little did I know that I would have to lose my literal vision to regain a true vision of peace, one rooted in the soul. The realization that external reality is a reflection of inner experiences brought me immense freedom, liberating me from limiting beliefs, projections, and judgments of both myself and others and giving me a deeper understanding of myself and my interactions with the world.

The running joke for my entire life has been that,

as Palestinians, we don't have a country because there are too many leaders and not enough followers. Each of us has our vision of what needs to be done. But over time, I've come to see this isn't just a Palestinian story—it's a human one. Around the world, we are conditioned by systems, schools, and institutions to forget that we are each born to lead and sovereign over our own destiny. And so we stay stuck in the waiting room—waiting for the Messiah, the hero, the perfect leader who will fix things, bring peace, or take responsibility for the mess we're in. We wait, all the while carrying within us the very spark we keep expecting from someone else.

Through this journey, I came to see something that challenged everything I had once believed. I learned that the roles of teacher and student are neither fixed nor separate. They are fluid, interchangeable, and—at times—illusionary. We hold onto them to feel secure in our place in the world.

I also discovered that within each of us lies the capacity for infinite expansion of consciousness. When we stop assigning authority solely to those outside of us and, instead, begin listening inward, we realize that the teacher is already here. And the student? She never stops learning—but she must learn to trust her own wisdom too.

Each of us has a vision that is unique to the specific soul experience we came here to have. It isn't about anyone else or whether they approve of this vision, like it, or follow it. Because soul visions can be shared, but they can't be imposed or manipulated. As such, my soul vision is mine, belonging to me and no one else, as I perceive the world from the perspective of my specific human experience. It is special, not because it is better than anyone else's, but because it is uniquely mine. All human interactions are based on love, attention, attraction, and repulsion. I may love, I hate, I like, I follow, I criticize others, but all I am really doing is loving, hating, liking, following, or criticizing myself. "Me" is all there is, whether I accept it or not.

Enough. Enough of this following, liking, loving, approving, hating, and criticizing. This is not what it's about. It is all about my experience and your experience—and, by extension, my understanding of my experience and your understanding of your experience. These elements may intersect somewhere, sometimes, but we do not need to manipulate, impose, or obligate, even when they don't. We can welcome differences of perspective.

The world likes clear definitions. It likes certainty, clarity, and clean-cut labels. People want an answer that fits neatly into their worldview, a response that makes sense to them. Are you Israeli or Palestinian? Muslim or secular? A peace activist or a nationalist? I have been asked these questions more times than I can count. They want to know where I stand so they can place me on their mental map of who is on which side.

There was a time when I thought I had to choose.

When I thought that, to have peace and belong somewhere, I needed to simplify myself, to align with one identity while rejecting the other. I thought I had to make a choice about what version of history I would align myself with and fit myself into the categories given to me because the world had no patience for complexity. But healing has taught me that I am not divided—I am whole. The world may try to place us in categories, but our deepest truth is beyond labels. My existence defies these binaries.

Wholeness is not something granted by a government, a passport, or a flag. It is not determined by what others call us, how they define us, or what histories they choose to recognize. Wholeness is something we must reclaim from within. True peace came not from choosing one half of myself over the other; it came from embracing the totality of my experience.

I have learned that the most radical thing I can do is refuse to be divided, to stand in my truth and hold my full identity without apology. To be Palestinian does not mean I am not Israeli. To be Israeli does not erase my Palestinian roots. To love my people does not mean I cannot believe in peace. To believe in peace does not mean I must ignore injustice.

There is power in embracing the contradictions and liberation in refusing to let the world's definitions define us. And so, I learned to stand comfortably as I was, between worlds, within worlds, beyond worlds. Doing so gets even more interesting when we have interactions with the "other" and learn that they are going through a similar process, only with a completely different understanding and complexity. That's where we get lost. That's where the conflict is.

One of the most difficult lessons I learned in this process was that pain exists on all sides of a given conflict. There is Jewish trauma from the Holocaust. There is Palestinian trauma from the Nakba. There are inherited fears and wounds of both peoples, and, whether or not we acknowledge them, these histories live inside of us.

I spent much of my life resisting this truth, fearing that recognizing the pain of the so-called other would somehow diminish my own. I feared that if I acknowledged Jewish suffering, it would be mistaken for justifying Palestinian oppression. I feared that holding space for both traumas meant betraying my own people. But pain is not a competition.

For too long, we have been locked in a cycle of suffering, each side arguing over whose wounds are deeper, whose history is more tragic, and whose loss is more deserving of recognition. It is as if justice could be measured in suffering, as if pain could be weighed against pain.

Healing is not about proving who has suffered more. It is about recognizing that suffering is shared, and that shared pain can become a foundation for shared healing. This does not mean erasing differences, nor does it mean ignoring systems of oppression that continue to cause harm. But it does mean that, if we are ever to find peace, we must stop dehumanizing each other's grief. We must stop believing that acknowledging another's pain erases our own. Pain expands the longer it is ignored. It festers in silence, and then it transforms into resentment, rage, and fear that are passed from one generation to the next. But when pain is acknowledged—fully, openly—it loses its power to control us.

I saw this truth most clearly within myself. For years, I had carried so much anger—at history, injustice, and the way the world refused to see my people's suffering. But beneath that anger was grief. And beneath that grief was fear. I feared I would always be unseen, that I would always be fighting to prove my existence, and that healing was not possible. But healing *is* possible. It begins with the willingness to see not only our own wounds but also those of the people we have been taught to see as enemies.

While the dynamics I speak of are present in many human stories and collective struggles, my soul's calling is to focus on one in particular: the conflict between Palestinians and Israelis. It's the ground I was born into and the wound I was entrusted to help tend. Nowhere is the Drama Triangle cycle more evident than in the Israeli-Palestinian conflict, where history, trauma, and power dynamics have solidified these roles:

Palestinians are often cast as perpetual

victims, expected to suffer, endure, and resist but rarely expected to lead or define their own future outside of oppression. Their pain is real, but the world often frames them as powerless, reinforcing a narrative that strips them of agency.

Israelis are placed into the role of perpetrators or defenders, either seen as oppressors who perpetuate violence or as a people whose survival depends on military dominance. The trauma of the Holocaust fuels a deep fear of annihilation, justifying a defensive posture that often leads to further cycles of violence.

The international community steps in as the rescuer but often in ways that reinforce dependency rather than empowerment. Global interventions tend to either enable oppression (through military aid and political alliances) or reinforce victimhood (through conditional aid that keeps people reliant rather than sovereign).

These roles are not only imposed from the outside but also internalized by those within the conflict. The result? Stagnation, repetition, and entrapment, as each side justifies its actions based on past wounds, holding onto its role as if letting go would mean betraying history. Each side fears that, without these identities, it would lose its narrative, its legitimacy, and its very sense of self.

This conflict is not just about land. It is about identity—about who we believe we are and what roles we believe we must play. As long as we remain in these roles, we remain trapped. In this intricate conflict, every aspect of life is inherently political, from the air we breathe to the choices we make. And yet, there comes a moment when we must accept accountability. We are ultimately responsible for our words, actions, and decisions. It is time to release the grip of victimhood—on both sides. Let us stop the competition of suffering.

Today, this crisis and ensuing war cast a deep shadow over our time. We are engulfed in the darkness of relentless killing, unbearable loss, and the unraveling of the very frameworks meant to uphold our shared humanity. The international language of rights and protection feels hollow against the weight of this suffering. It is as if the moral fabric that once tethered us is tearing in real time.

And yet, in this darkness, we are not powerless. As we move forward—individually and collectively—we must continue to hold each other. We must listen, resisting the pull of dehumanization and, instead, nurturing the fragile, life-affirming threads of connection that still remain. In sharing our stories and truths, we create space not only to witness one another's pain but to remember our own dignity.

Even now—especially now—story becomes a form of resistance, and healing is an act of collective memory. It is through shared remembrance that we may still find our way—not back to what was but forward to something more whole, more just, and more deeply human.

At the same time, we must be honest about the

dynamics of power. Israel holds the upper hand, even as it denies its role as an occupying force as well as the oppression it enacts. The narrative that the occupation of Palestine is necessary for Jewish safety is outdated and ultimately harmful to both peoples. Acknowledging this truth is not about blame—it's about opening the door to a different path.

I believe that both the Jews and the Palestinians are courageous adversaries. They are noble enemies who have chosen to confront violence, chaos, and suffering while the world watches with polarizing views. Are they with us, so against them? Or are they against us, so with them? This vortex of religious and patriarchal structures is in desperate need of divine femininity, and it is time for a change. What path will we choose? Will we continue to avoid addressing the issues at hand? Or will we courageously and openly acknowledge and confront reality?

The essence of the problem is the betrayal of our soul and collective spirit, which affects all, Jews and Palestinians alike. Are we ready to finally confront this truth? Can we finally start a transformation of this conflict from within?

As we collectively navigate these challenging times, let us return to the wisdom of the feminine as a vital force within us all. In a world long dominated by the wounded masculine—driven by control, competition, and separation—the feminine invites us back to the heart: to intuition, care, interconnectedness, and deep listening. Our true selves are not found in one polarity or the other but in the integration of both. For many of us, reconnecting with the feminine is the doorway that leads us home.

Equanimity involves striking an inner and outer balance, being attuned to the world around us and maintaining inner peace. It requires acknowledging the complexities of conflicts and striving to understand the perspectives of all parties involved. Equanimity allows us to see beyond surface-level appearances to question prevailing narratives and seek a deeper truth.

Genuine equanimity is attained by embracing our emotions fully, a lesson I learned firsthand during my two years without eyesight. It involves recognizing and overcoming our biases and prejudices, accepting that conflict is an inherent part of human nature but that it need not define us. Even in conflict, we can choose to remain grounded, seek understanding, and cultivate compassion.

It's time to confront these issues head-on and move away from walking on eggshells. Let's address the realities and complexities of the Israeli-Palestinian conflict, recognizing that Israel can no longer sell the religious narrative it has clung to for seventy-five years. One nation cannot occupy and suppress another and still claim to be a true democracy.

At the heart of this issue, one of the world's most enduring conflicts, we find an opportunity to let us bring the light of peace forward. Our vision calls for us to embrace the shared humanity of both Palestinians and Israelis, recognizing that the light within each person shines with equal brilliance.

We cannot seek peace only as an external goal; we must cultivate it within ourselves and extend it outward. Through dialogue, understanding, and compassion, we can dismantle the walls of separation and build bridges of connection. The reclamation of feminine power plays a crucial role here, as it brings nurturing, empathy, and collaborative problem-solving to the forefront of our efforts.

In this sacred journey, the sisterhood of peace emerges as a powerful force—one I've had the honor of cultivating and witnessing over time. It's not just an abstract vision but a lived reality that has taken form in retreats held in Cyprus, in Greece, and in gatherings on the land of our shared homeland. Women from both sides—Palestinian and Israeli—have come together in these spaces with open hearts, transcending the boundaries that have long divided our communities.

In circle, we cry, listen, and remember. This sisterhood touches and heals not only the individual but also the collective wound. It reminds us that healing is possible when we dare to show up with tenderness, to sit in truth, and to see one another, not as enemies or opposites, but as reflections of a shared longing for peace.

Together, we dance with the light, activating the gift of peace within ourselves and our communities. By embracing our true nature and reclaiming our feminine power, we transform the illusion of separation into a profound realization of our oneness. In the spirit of unity, let us light the way toward a future where peace reigns over conflict and love triumphs over hate.

Bridging the divides may seem insurmountable. But our personal growth and connections with others who share our vision can give us hope. We can navigate this complex landscape with dedication to healing, understanding, and inner freedom. We can work together toward a future where humanity prevails.

And so, I carry my vision forward with my heart. I choose to see the truth, even when it is inconvenient. I choose to witness the erased, the forgotten, and the silenced. Because to see is not just a gift—it is a responsibility.

A responsibility to remember.

A responsibility to resist.

A responsibility to reclaim what has been taken.

I came here for this human experience with three ingredients: the essence of love, the power of choice, and the responsibility for my life choices. It is time for me to acknowledge it, articulate it, and live by it.

"There is no way to peace—
peace is the way."

~ Thich Nhat Hanh

chapter nine

THE MISSING ELEMENT

"She is here to bring peace…" These words echoed around me, especially in my first field mission in Burundi at the age of thirty-one. One participant in the workshop I was facilitating called me "Amahoro," the one who brings peace. This resonated with a truth that surpassed mere existence. It wasn't just about equipping people with tools, as I once had believed. It was about embodying peace by living it and breathing it into every interaction and every moment.

For years, I believed that change had to come from the outside—from leadership, from institutions, from legal frameworks. But the more I engaged in peace work, the more I saw that no policy, no treaty, no declaration could heal the wounds of a people if those wounds remained unaddressed.

We cannot build peace on wounded ground. We must tend to the unseen, heal what history has buried, and awaken the soul of our becoming. Leaving my home country at the age of nineteen marked the beginning of an unpredictable journey that transcended borders and conventional paths. As I set out into the wider world, I carried with me a deep yearning to understand not just the external landscapes I encountered but also the intricate terrains of my own soul.

I witnessed the same patterns repeating: the same conflicts reigniting, the same negotiations stalling, and the same injustices persisting. The more I saw this, the more I wondered why. Why do peace agreements collapse? Why do movements for justice sometimes breed new cycles of division? Why does history seem destined to repeat itself?

The answer wasn't just political. It was psychological, spiritual, and even existential. What if peace building wasn't just about resolving political disputes but about breaking generational cycles of suffering? In that case, true peace would require us to transform not just our societies but ourselves. True peace would require deep, ancestral, soul-centered healing.

If we consider peace as something that's not just about politics but also about human connection, our understanding of the concept itself is transformed. Peace building wouldn't, then, start in government halls, but in the spaces where people learn to see one another's humanity. Losing my eyesight forced me to confront my own inner conflicts—the invisible wounds I carried, the ancestral traumas woven into my identity, and the fears that shaped how I saw the world. Then, as I healed, I began to see more clearly just how the world's conflicts are reflections of our unresolved inner pain.

We externalize what we have not healed within, and nations mirror the traumas of their people. Therefore, the violence we see in the world echoes the suffering we hold inside. That's the thing: unless we tend to that suffering, no treaty will hold, no ceasefire will endure, and no border will bring peace. This realization changed everything.

I finally understood that peace couldn't be imposed from the outside. It had to be activated from within. Then came October 7.

The horror of that day, and the violence that followed, shattered any illusion that the systems in place—political, humanitarian, diplomatic—were equipped to hold the weight of our collective pain. The international community responded too late, too politically, too cautiously. All the while, lives were lost and communities destroyed. The trauma deepened on both sides.

What we saw was not just the failure of politics. It was the failure of imagination, of addressing the roots beneath the fire. Trauma left unhealed will always find expression—often through destruction. It affirmed what I had already come to believe: Peace is not just a political process. It is a soul-centered practice.

The world seeks resolution and clear answers in the form of treaties, borders, and diplomacy. It yearns for a final decision that will close the chapter of the Israeli-Palestinian conflict. So leaders negotiate agreements, governments propose solutions, and the international community debates policies, all in search of something definitive, like a line drawn on a map or a signature on a dotted line. The world asks for a fixed outcome when true peace is a living thing that cannot be manufactured.

Peace cannot be imposed through declarations. It is an ongoing process, a daily act of quiet courage. It is found in the spaces between us—in the way we listen, in the way we refuse to dehumanize, in the way we choose dialogue over silence and understanding over fear—and it must be made again and again.

History has shown us countless peace agreements that were signed with great ceremony and lauded as milestones in the path toward reconciliation. And yet, how many of these agreements have truly led to lasting peace? Peace on paper is meaningless if the people still live in fear. If communities remain trapped in grief, anger, and the wounds of past violence, no border drawn on a map can prevent the next war from coming in spite of surface-level efforts. To truly build peace, we must stop treating it as a political transaction and start seeing it as a human transformation.

Beneath the surface of every geopolitical conflict is an unseen battlefield: the historical trauma carried in the hearts and bodies of those who have suffered. Most peace agreements collapse not because the terms were flawed, but because they failed to address this deeper issue. Nations do not move forward simply because documents are signed.

This is the missing piece that politicians rarely speak of. They negotiate the external, but the real war exists in the very cells of our being. Science confirms what our ancestors have always known: trauma is passed down through generations. Epigenetic research shows that it is not just psychological—it is biologically encoded into us. We carry the unspoken grief of our ancestors in our bones, their fears woven into the fibers of our nervous system.

I, too, carried more than my own suffering. I carried the silent grief of my grandparents, who lived through the Nakbah and watched their world change overnight. Within me, I carried the quiet rage of my parents, who had learned to navigate a state that treated them as second-class citizens. I carried the confusion of a generation born into contradictions, struggling to piece together an identity from fragments of history. But if trauma can be passed down, so can healing.

I spent years trying to force myself into answers that did not fit because the world wants fixed identities and definitive truths. But healing is about making peace with contradiction. To be human is to be paradoxical, and control is an illusion. To hold grief and joy at the same time. To feel both anger and compassion in the same breath. To acknowledge wounds without being defined by them.

We're taught that remaining steadfast in our convictions is strength, that loosening our grip is akin to giving up and risking the loss of what little power we still have. I had gripped so tightly to narratives that helped me make sense of my suffering, convincing myself that if I could just find the right cause, the right argument, the right resolution, then everything would finally align. But in time, I began to see the truth: some of the things I clung to the most were the very things holding me back.

There is a deep comfort in righteous suffering. It gives us clarity and a sense of purpose. It tells us who we are, who the enemy is, and what the fight is about. We build entire identities around what has been taken from us, forgetting that who we are is greater than any imposed label. But suffering can also become a prison we do not know how to leave, and there is a danger in defining oneself solely through oppression.

For much of my life, I resisted fully owning my Palestinian identity because I had been conditioned to believe it meant victimhood. Our story—when it's acknowledged at all—is usually one of loss, about a people who continue to endure in spite of having been wronged. That suffering is real and cannot be minimized or erased. But suffering is not our only story. To be Palestinian is not only to have lost; it is also to have survived, to have created, to have loved, to have lived.

Sure, we crave closure, clarity, and an endpoint. But, in reality, some stories will always be unfinished.

For so long, I feared that embracing my Palestinian identity meant embracing only grief. What I failed to see was that to claim an identity is not to be defined by its pain, but by its wholeness. So I had to ask myself: Who am I beyond my suffering? What does it mean to be Palestinian outside of struggle? Who am I when I am not fighting for recognition? Who am I beyond what history has done to me?

For so long, my identity had been shaped by what had been taken from me. I understood myself through loss—of land, of belonging, of recognition. But healing means stepping into a new way of being that is not defined by pain.

Releasing our grip on our pain does not mean erasing the past—it means making space for something new. It means reclaiming joy, love, and the fullness of identity beyond trauma. I could be both Palestinian and free, both wounded and whole, both hopeful and grieving, both a seeker of justice and a believer in healing. In that in-between space, I began to see myself clearly, not as broken or divided, but as layered and whole. None of these identities canceled each other out. And it was in this quiet reckoning that I discovered the most radical act of all: radical self-acceptance as an act of resistance.

True reconciliation begins within. For years, I had felt like I was at war within my own skin. One part of me pulled toward belonging and another toward resistance. One part sought recognition while another rejected the structures that refused to see me. The moment I accepted all parts of myself—the Israeli passport I hold, the Palestinian roots I claim, the contradictions within me—I stopped fighting against myself. I no longer saw myself as fragmented.

Reconciliation with the world begins with reconciliation with the self. I cannot ask for peace in the world if I do not hold peace within me. When I do, I am free because I am no longer relying on validation to exist or needing to prove my identity to anyone. I no longer needed to choose between the pieces of myself.

Healing means breaking ancestral cycles and refusing to pass down wounds that were never ours to begin with, but this does not mean forgetting history. It does not mean moving on without justice. Instead, we simply choose not to let history define us or dictate our future. Healing is not about forgetting the past—it is about choosing not to be controlled by it.

When we heal, we do not just heal for ourselves. We heal for those who came before us and for those who will come after. Our pain is interconnected, and so is our healing. Healing ourselves is what stops pain from being passed like an inheritance. That's why choosing healing—personally, spiritually, politically— is one of the most radical acts we can take. To heal is to disrupt the cycle of violence that history has placed in our hands. It is to reclaim our agency and say: "I will not pass this suffering forward."

This is why healing is so deeply tied to justice, which requires truth-telling, witnessing, and making space for grief and repair. The greatest threat to systems built on division is not war. Healing is what dismantles the narratives that fuel conflict and allows us to see beyond our inherited roles of victim and oppressor, enemy and ally. Healing forces us to confront the stories we have been told about who we are and who we are supposed to hate.

It is easy to stay in the roles we know. Remaining the victim gives us identity. Becoming the rescuer makes us feel important. Being the perpetrator allows us to justify our actions through history. What is hard is stepping out of the cycle entirely, choosing healing when the world expects us to grip onto our pain. As a global community, we must stop waiting for saviors and become active participants in change, encouraging communities to reclaim their power. Instead of waiting for the world to change, we must decide for ourselves that we will no longer live by the scripts we were given.

When we, as individuals, commit to both inner and outer transformation, systems are rebuilt on equity rather than control. Once we heal, we cannot be controlled in the same way because, when we heal, we see differently. We see that liberation is not about clarity. It is about embracing the fullness of who we are, even when it does not fit neatly into categories. And our liberation is bound together.

If we want true liberation, we have to move beyond our adopted identities and reclaim a sense of self that is not rooted in oppression, but in creation and possibility. For me, that meant being defined not by what I had lost, but by what I was building. That clarity only emerged when my vision loss caused the outer world to fade, forcing me to turn inward. In that darkness, I began to imagine a new way of seeing, a new way of being.

In the ruins of uncertainty, I founded Peace Activation in October 2023. Both an organization and a methodology, it was born in response to the moment I found myself in. I held the belief that peace is not just a political process but a soul-centered practice, a lived experience that begins in the body, in community, and in truth-telling. Peace Activation is meant to bring about remembrance that healing and justice begin within, knowing that we cannot rebuild externally what is broken internally.

Rather than a response to policy gaps, it is a framework for those who know that the future will not be built by power alone but by those who dare to stay human in the face of inhumanity. It is for those who are ready to walk together and willing to grieve, listen, and reconcile within themselves and across divides. Because if we do not shift how we relate to ourselves, to each other, and to the past, we will keep repeating it.

Real peace cannot be legislated without healing. It must rise from within us before it can ripple through our relationships and transform the systems we have considered unshakable. So, as we move forward—individually and collectively—we must hold each other with fierce tenderness. We must find the courage to tell the truth as well as the humility to listen deeply. We must remember that, in sharing our stories, we make space for each other to be seen, even in the darkest of times. We must ask: How do we honor the past without letting it control us? How do we acknowledge trauma without using it as a way to justify harm?

This is what Peace Activation offers: not an escape from the dark, but a path through it—together. It is not merely about mediation, policy change, or dialogue. It is about deep, embodied healing that honors the past while building something new.

History does not have to dictate the future. As nations, we can stop repeating the cycles of oppression we have inherited. Peace Activation was born from this understanding as more than an organization. Rather, it is a movement that invites us to transcend narratives of victimhood and separation. A movement for those who believe that true peace is an inside-out process and are ready to step beyond blame and into responsibility. A movement for those who understand that the world will only change when we do because healing, like peace, requires action.

Peace Activation is a call to those who believe

that peace is not just an end goal but a way of being. It is an ongoing practice of unlearning separation and re-learning connection. It is the courage to look at our own pain, transform it, and no longer let it dictate how we show up in the world.

I believe in the kind of peace work that does not just ask for ceasefires but for heart-opening and emotional reconciliation. And so I choose to move forward—with grief and awareness but without bitterness or hatred. The deep knowing that my existence is neither an apology nor a contradiction is a truth that no border can contain.

When my vision returned and I revisited the same space where I once danced in darkness as my friend Aisha played DJ for me, I was struck by the vastness of the surrounding room. There was plenty of empty space to dance and move around. I had been worried I would fall or collide with something, but the space was wide open, with no chairs or tables blocking the way. It was vast and ready for my movements. All along, the space I possessed seemed infinite compared to the tiny corner I had once confined myself to. We imprison ourselves within the walls of our own doubts and fears, when, in reality, the world around us is much more expansive than we imagine.

But sometimes, the expanses of the world around us also open us up to unsettling realities. One truth in particular was notably painful for me. For twenty-five years, I had seen my role as a peace builder, a mediator, and someone who could help others navigate conflict. I believed that if I worked hard enough, spoke to enough people, and held enough dialogues, I could bridge the divides that seemed insurmountable. But there is a danger in peacework that is rooted in fixing, in stepping into the savior role.

In this work, I had not only been a rescuer—I had also been a victim of my own need to be needed. This is the danger of the rescuer role. It makes us feel indispensable, when, in reality, no one can save another. It convinces us that our worth is in helping rather than simply being. It creates dependency rather than empowerment. This realization shattered me—because I saw that I had been reinforcing the very cycles I sought to break.

I had spent years playing the rescuer in my relationships—always stepping in, always trying to fix, always carrying burdens that were never mine to carry. I was the peace builder, the mediator, the one who believed I could help others heal their conflicts. And yet, in my blindness, I was forced to confront the uncomfortable curiosities that this work brought up in me.

Did I step into conflict resolution because I genuinely wanted to empower others, or was it because it gave me a sense of importance? Did I try to heal others because I saw their potential, or because I was avoiding my own pain? Was I here to hold space, or was I trying to control outcomes? Did I believe in peace, or did I believe in my role as the one who could bring it about? Who was I really doing this work for?

I had to unlearn the belief that healing meant saving others or that my value came from what I could fix. True healing is never about saving someone else. It is about creating space for people to reclaim their own narratives, their own power, and their own healing. It is about empowerment, not intervention.

There is an ego trap in activism and peace building. We want to be the ones who affect change, but healing does not happen when we insert ourselves into others' journeys. It happens when we step back and hold space without ownership, recognizing that we are not the center of anyone else's healing but our own. We are not here to liberate others; we are here to remind them of their own liberation.

True peace activism is not about seeking recognition, proving our goodness, or making ourselves the story. It is about choosing to show up, even when no one is watching, to ensure that healing, justice, and dignity are accessible to all. It's not about being the one who fixes the world, but about doing the work that must be done, holding complexity without collapsing into fear or righteousness. It's how we breathe, how we walk, and how we relate to one another when the world is burning. It is about aligning our values with our actions—not as an identity, but as a practice.

Many spiritual communities speak of "rising above conflict" and "not engaging in negativity." They speak of detachment as a path to peace, of staying "neutral" as a form of wisdom. But spirituality without responsibility is just another escape because true healing requires engagement, not avoidance. The bridge between spirituality and activism is clarity, humility, and self-awareness.

So, how can spiritual seekers engage in peace activism without reinforcing oppression? How can we be of service without centering ourselves in someone else's struggle? The answer is responsibility. We must take radical ownership of our healing and our contributions to cycles of pain.

Peace is not the absence of conflict. We break inherited cycles of suffering by choosing, every day, to embody the change we wish to see. We get to choose how we show up in the world, how we listen, and whether we create spaces where others can heal too. Healing does not mean rejecting the world's suffering because it is uncomfortable—it means holding space for it, witnessing it, and working toward its transformation.

To heal does not mean to bypass pain. It means to face it, to meet it where it lives and sit with it without turning away. When we stop outsourcing the work of reconciliation to politicians and begin doing the work within ourselves, we acknowledge the wars we carry inside ourselves and can finally dare to lay down our arms.

There is no true neutrality in systems of

oppression. To claim neutrality in the face of injustice is a privileged act. It is to align, passively, with the status quo. To be silent in the face of suffering is complicity.

We cannot meditate our way out of oppression or manifest our way out of harm. Healing demands participation and courageous presence as we move beyond theory and into action, taking the wisdom we have gained from our personal transformation and applying it to the world around us. Spirituality, at its core, is not about retreating from the world. It is about engaging with it differently, with clarity, integrity, and love that is not just an emotion but an action. We must do the work.

We live in a world that often demands division and certainty. We are told to pick a side, to define ourselves in opposition to others, to seek clarity in black-and-white terms. Yet, just as we must learn to live with personal uncertainty, we must learn to live with polit-ical uncertainty as well. There will not always be clarity or closure. And yet, we move forward.

The work of peace does not move from war to resolution in a single, linear arc. It is layered, fragile, and messy, demanding patience in the absence of immediate results and faith in the process, even when progress is invisible. It is about planting seeds that may not bloom in our lifetime but must be planted anyway.

The way we learn to hold our own contradictions and navigate our own inner conflicts is the way we will show up for the world's conflicts. The way we heal ourselves is the way we heal each other. The way we make peace within is the way we build peace outside of us. Healing is not separate from justice. Peace is not separate from identity—there is no distinction, and there never was.

I once believed that healing meant reaching a place of certainty. That peace—both personal and political—meant resolution, a point at which all questions would be answered, all pain would be transformed, and all conflicts would dissolve into understanding. So, when I regained my eyesight, I believed I had completed something—that I had crossed a threshold, endured a test, and now stood firmly on the other side.

We like to think of peace in this way—as a place we will one day reach, a fixed moment in time when the fighting stops, justice is restored, and suffering is no more. But peace is not a final destination, and the healing never ends; it is an ongoing, ever-deepening process. Just as healing is the continuous unfolding of self, peace is the continuous unfolding of humanity.

There is no moment when we can declare ourselves whole and close the door on pain. Healing is a path full of twists and turns, revealing new terrain just when we think we have mapped it all out. It is a continuous process of unfolding, an invitation to engage with the world in a new way, to see beyond what is visible, and to trust in the unseen.

I have learned that neither healing nor peace is a static state. They are practices that require us to show up again and again, even when the path is unclear and the world feels unyielding, even when we are asked to step forward in faith before the ground beneath us is visible.

True transformation does not come from force or resistance, but from presence—the willingness to sit with what is, hold complexity, and release the need for immediate answers. The same is true for peace. These processes require surrender, the deep listening to our bodies, our histories, and the spaces of silence within us.

The personal is always political. My journey of losing and regaining vision was never just about my body—it was about breaking through inherited trauma, silence, and imposed narratives. It was about seeing in a way I never had before—not just with my eyes but with my heart, my history, and my understanding of power and healing.

There is a reason why the world does not encourage deep healing. To heal is to wake up, to wake up is to see clearly, and to see clearly is to recognize the structures that keep us in suffering. To reclaim peace—not as a distant ideal, but as a lived practice—is a radical refusal to accept oppression as fate.

To heal in a world that profits from division is an act of defiance because it disrupts cycles of harm and interrupts the transmission of trauma, fear, and inherited hatred. When we heal, we step outside of the narratives that have been forced upon us. We reclaim our power to define our own path, to choose peace, not as submission, but as a form of radical self-ownership.

But healing is not just about finding peace within. It is about bringing that peace into the world. To love in a world that thrives on separation is an act of courage, just as to heal in a world that does not want us whole is an act of power. And power—when used with awareness and integrity—can be the force that dismantles harm and builds something new in its place.

Peace is not an external goal. It is not something that will one day arrive. It is an internal state of being, lived outwardly and practiced daily. It is the way we show up in our conversations, in our relationships, and in the way we treat those who are different from us. It is in the way we listen, the way we make space, the way we choose understanding over division. We do not wait for peace; we embody it. The work is not done. It is just beginning.

"*The cave you fear to enter
holds the treasure you seek.*"

~ *Joseph Campbell*

chapter ten

THE PATH OF THE SOUL

Throughout my healing journey, friends and strangers continually asserted how resilient I was and how impressed they were with how I was coping. My answer? Resilience, the toughness that comes from all the difficulties we face, is the way we take a deep breath and continue living, ready to confront the next hardship. And resilience is everywhere we look when we are ready to tap into it.

It's not that I am not faced with challenges. Rather, my perspective on those challenges has changed. I always knew I had resilience, having grown up in one conflict zone and worked in many others. But this new resilience of mine didn't have the same tough look to it. It wasn't about fighting life to survive; it was about embracing life to thrive.

The key to this viewpoint was a deeper, more active form of self-care that was linked to self-responsibility rather than the passive expectation for external forms of care from family or friends. I had learned to take time to sit with myself, allocating attention and appreciation to what I was going through. I moved more in acceptance rather than arguing about what is. I developed a new perspective on life, which was softer, slower, and sweeter.

People tend to find resilience in worst-case, nightmarish situations, which often connect us to a level of strength we didn't even know existed. I once met a woman in the Congo at the end of my field mission who had to leave her town and run from the conflict when her husband was taken by the rebels, leaving her alone with her children. Her parents were in another town, all of them dislocated, separated from their place of origin. Yet, with a smile on her face, she told me how proud she was of at least having kept her children together throughout the war. Her hope of one day being reunited with the whole family kept her alive.

Nor will I forget the story of a mother in the Palestinian-occupied territories who lost her daughter at a checkpoint. For some unapparent reason, the soldiers at the Israeli checkpoint had been holding everyone back, and she wasn't able to cross the border in time to get to the hospital to deliver her baby. The arbitrary nature of the conflict was manifest, both parties having to deny the humanity of the other so that they could maintain the violence, even though they knew deep inside it didn't make sense.

That mother, aching with grief over the loss of her daughter, had tears in her eyes as she told her story. Yet, she also smiled as she shared that she kept choosing life, continuing to cook and care for her other children. She held deep hope that one day she would experience peace in her home while, at the same time, acknowledging her pain.

These stories and others that are too long to recall here have taught me how resilience is always available to all people, anywhere in the world. I had witnessed resilience unfold throughout my career across various conflict zones in Africa, the Middle East, and Southeast Asia. Yet, here I found myself not just observing others' stories of strength but also living my own. Experiencing resilience in my own body, mind, and spirit brought about a profound shift in my understanding of self.

In parallel to these experiences, I had long operated as a people pleaser, driven by a deep-seated desire to accommodate and uplift those around me. Whether with loved ones or new acquaintances, my focus was always on making others feel valued and supported. I thrived on sharing joy and meeting perceived needs, whether through a smile, a comforting gesture, or nourishing meals. I became adept at observing social dynamics, anticipating needs, and ensuring everyone felt attended to—an approach that brought validation and recognition. Yet, amidst this outward focus, I inadvertently neglected the most crucial person: myself.

Now, as the journey deepens and I look deeper within myself, I return to a familiar place. Grief has a way of circling back, not always in the same form, but in familiar textures: uncertainty, vulnerability, the ache of not knowing what comes next. This time, it isn't just personal. It's collective.

What is unfolding in Gaza and across this deeply fractured land pierces the deepest parts of me. This is not distant news; it is a living wound, ancestral and immediate. The grief I carry lives in my bones, my memory, and my generations. To witness this scale of devastation is to confront the unbearable. But healing and horror often arrive intertwined. In a world numbed by repetition, we must keep in mind that staying present is a radical act. To choose feeling in spite of the pain and remain human in spite of the confusion and discomfort are even more so.

Grief is not a sign that we are broken. It is evidence that we are awake and that we care. And it is often in these vulnerable thresholds—where loss and possibility meet—that resilience is born again as devotion to what comes next.

I continue to sit with sadness, hope, and unanswered expectations. None of it is neatly resolved. But the way I share has shifted. What once felt urgent to speak out in circles and gatherings has slowly turned inward. My sharing has become less public, less rooted in physical spaces, and more present through the screen—in messages, quiet reflections, and, now, this book.

After two years of processing out loud, I felt called to write. In the written word, I've found comfort and an intimacy that allows me to go deeper into my sensitivity, to listen more closely to the texture of the story, and to gently make sense of it. Writing invites me to reread the journey as it unfolds, to offer meaning where there is confusion and connection where there is aching silence. It has become a sacred thread, a way to say you are not alone in your loss, your becoming, or your longing to make sense of what feels senseless.

What I feel now is braided with uncertainty, not just for myself but for the world. The unbearable suffering unfolding in Gaza, the rising despair across the land, and the deafening silence in so many places— all of it lives in me. It calls up the same questions I asked when I lost my vision: how do we live when we cannot see what comes next?

Peace Activation was born in this tension. It is rooted in the belief that we must hold personal and collective grief together, that healing is not separate from justice, and that peace is not a destination, but a daily, courageous act. In this time of deep rupture, I return to the practice of listening—to the land, the body, and the spaces between the words. Writing is how I now hold the fire. It's how I remain in the question. And, in that question, I find my way back to hope.

In the depths of my blindness, I questioned whether I would ever see again. The world had disappeared into darkness, and I had no evidence or certainty that my sight would ever return. I had to trust in what was unseen, and that trust did not come easily. It required surrender, letting go of control, and the willingness to believe in something beyond my immediate reality.

In both my personal healing process and in the context of war, there is a natural tendency to seek resolution because the mind craves answers and the heart craves closure. We want to believe that suffering has meaning, that every loss will be accounted for, and that justice will arrive in a neat and timely manner. But I have learned that not all suffering has an immediate answer and not every story has a neat resolution. Some wounds cannot be explained or justified. They simply exist. We do not always have to fix, resolve, or explain our pain. Sometimes, we just need to sit with it.

When I look at the state of the world, the weight of history, and the scars left behind by conflict, it is easy to feel that peace is impossible. When the wounds are so deep, it's easy to think they'll never heal. Peace, like sight, requires us to believe before we see. Even when the present moment tells us otherwise, faith gives us the willingness to move forward, to build, plant, and dream—not because we have proof that peace will come, but because we refuse to accept that it won't.

Faith is not about certainty. It is about choosing

to believe in possibility even when the evidence is not yet visible. This lesson extends beyond my personal healing into the way I see the world. The same trust I had to cultivate in my own recovery is the trust I must hold for the possibility of peace. This is one of the hardest lessons because uncertainty is uncomfortable. It asks us to let go of control and to sit with what is rather than what we wish it to be.

I take comfort in the certainties that exist amidst the uncertainties I can't control. I know for certain that contributing to something and being of service is my soul's calling—at least right now. I know, too, that love is the oxygen of the soul, just like dance is my soul's unique expression. I know that I have gone through so much transformation in these past two years and dropped so many layers of protection and ego— of who I have thought I should be and how I have thought I should behave. I know that, today, I feel I am a different person.

I have dropped the layer of the people pleaser, the woman in control, the planner, the organizer, the mother, the daughter, and the wife. These social identities are what I clung to for so long—particularly the professional ones: the consultant, the coach, the facilitator, the one who delivers the training, the knowledge, the skills, and the attitude shifts. But we are not meant to carry everything forever.

We are also not meant to grip onto pain as if it defines us. We are not meant to live only in the past nor only in the future but to be here—fully, presently—holding both what has been lost and what is yet to come. Letting go is not a betrayal, and releasing does not mean we no longer care. It means we trust that life moves forward, even when we do not have all the answers.

And so I choose to hold on—to what is sacred and what is true. And I choose to let go of the illusions and the weight that are no longer mine to carry. Because peace is not about certainty. It is about learning to stand in the unknown with an open heart and say: I am here. And that is enough.

None of my identities were available to me when it was just me and the dark. Blindly sitting or lying on the ground, I connected my heartbeat to the heartbeat of the earth. This was the only thing that could soothe me. It brought with it the self-responsibility to take action in response to my needs, rather than constantly prioritizing the needs of others, even when I wasn't asked to. That was the true gift—the gift of resilience and reconnecting with myself and my heart, gaining a deeper understanding of my own needs.

I learned to read these subtle messages by tuning into something other than my eyes, going deeper into my senses and my body. This shift allowed me to feel what was going on for me first and then apply that awareness to others as well, even without physically seeing them.

This is my passion now: to live from the soul and

share that way of being with others. Through Peace Activation, my teachings, my coaching, my retreats—and even around the dinner table with friends and family—I get to show up as who I truly am.

We don't know how strong we are until life brings us to the edge of what we think we can bear. Then, something ancient stirs—a hidden reservoir of strength we never knew existed. Not because we're fearless, but because we have no other choice. We survive. We rise. We remember.

Until that moment, we may drift in complacency, drowning in self-limiting beliefs about who we are and what we can do. But in crisis—when danger strikes, when loss empties us, when there is nothing left to lose—that is when our deepest strength awakens. That is when we step into the highest potential of who we came here to be.

I learned to slow down because I didn't have a choice. The process softened and sweetened me, shifting my focus from a goal-oriented life to soul-centered living. This is the invitation now—not just to survive but to become. To live from the soul. To rise from the ashes of what was and embody the strength, clarity, and peace we were always meant to carry. May your healing be your offering.

Peace is not something we wait for—it is something we activate, here and now, in the way we choose to see, to love, and to live. The dance begins when you take the first step.

A CALL TO ACTION: YOUR ROLE IN THIS JOURNEY

Healing does not stop with the self. It is not enough to transform internally and leave the world unchanged. The wisdom gained from suffering—whether personal or collective—carries a responsibility: to be shared, lived, and woven into the fabric of human connection.

What do we do with the truths we have unearthed? How do we ensure that our personal healing does not become an isolated act but ripples outward, dismantling the structures of harm?

This book is a call to embody peace, not just dream of it. To take the wisdom gained from darkness and illuminate the world, to personal relationships, political discourse, and collective healing.

The work of peace does not belong to politicians alone. It belongs to each of us in the way we show up in our daily lives. This is not just my journey. It is yours too. It is all of ours. If this book resonated with you—if you have ever felt caught between identities, if you have struggled to find your place in a world of conflict, if you believe that healing and peace must begin from within—then I invite you to take the next step.

We may not have the power to rewrite history, but we have the power to break inherited patterns. We may not be able to control global conflicts, but we can control how we respond to suffering—our own and others'. We may not have all the answers, but we can commit to asking better questions.

So I ask you: Where in your own life is there an unhealed conflict that still plays out in your thoughts and actions? What wounds—personal, historical, or collective—are you still holding onto? How might releasing them open a path to something new? How can you embody peace—not just as an idea but as a daily practice?

This is the work. This is the invitation.

Peace is not something we wait for. It is something we activate. Together, we can transform suffering into wisdom, division into connection, and darkness into light.

Are you ready to activate peace within yourself and in the world? It is not easy. It will ask everything of you. It will require you to let go of certainty, to step into the unknown, to trust in what you cannot yet see.

But this is how healing happens. This is how peace

begins. Not out there in some distant future. But here. With you. With us.

And so, the journey continues.

Join Peace Activation: the Soul-Centered Peace Movement

references

Patterns of Attachment: A Psychological Study of the Strange Situation by Mary D. S. Ainsworth

Isis Unveiled: A Master-Key to the Mysteries of Ancient and Modern Science and Theology by Helena Blavatsky

Attachment and Loss: Vol. 1. Attachment by John Bowlby

The Hero with a Thousand Faces by Joseph Campbell

The Hundredth Monkey by Ken Keyes Jr.

The Heroine's Journey: Woman's Quest for Wholeness by Maureen Murdock

The Gene Keys: Unlocking the Purpose Hidden in Your DNA by Richard Rudd

The Body Keeps the Score: Brain, Mind, and Body in the Healing of Trauma by Bessel van der Kolk

acknowledgments

Sincere gratitude to my mother, Naema, and my father, Mohamed Fathi—your love has been my root and my compass. To my sisters, Ghada and Abir, and my brothers, Abed and Rafi—thank you for being my anchors in every season and for holding me in ways both seen and unseen.

To my beloved Fabrice—your devotion and patience are my safe anchor. To our boys, Omram and Kyan—you are my greatest teachers and my joy.

To all my blood family and soul family and to the friends who supported me financially, logistically, and emotionally through the many turns of this journey—you made it possible for me to walk this path with both feet on the ground and my heart wide open.

To my dear friends Meg, Sophie, Aisha, Lena, Francesca, Claudia, Beatrice, Pauline, Claudine, Sandra, Dalit, Neslihan, Isabelle, and all the sisters of the

Rainbow Circle—your love, kindness, and presence have lit my path again and again.

To Toby, for your writing coaching—begun while I was still not seeing—and for the prompt that sparked this book into being. You helped me find my voice in the dark. To Amanda Johnson and the team at Awaken Village Press—thank you for walking beside me with such care and skill, bringing this book to its final destination.

To my teachers, healers, and guides—seen and unseen—who restored not only my vision but my faith.

To my companions in peace building—Palestinians, Israelis, and allies near and far—thank you for teaching me that dialogue is an act of love and that peace begins within the human heart.

And to the great mystery that carried me when I could not see my own way—thank you for reminding me that light is never lost.

And last but not least, to my reader—thank you for witnessing me. May you remember who you are, even in the darkest of times. *The light you're seeking is already within you.*

about the author

Eva Dalak is a coach, facilitator, and trainer dedicated to transforming conflict into possibility and pain into healing. With more than twenty-five years of experience in international development, women's empowerment, and peace building, she brings a trauma-informed and heart-centered approach to her work. As the founder of Peace Activation, Eva creates spaces where individuals and communities can reclaim their resilience, embody compassion, and activate peace from within. Her journey—bridging personal healing with collective transformation—inspires her mission to guide others toward lives rooted in wholeness and connection. Learn more at www.evadalak.me and www.peaceactivation.org.

www.ingramcontent.com/pod-product-compliance
Lightning Source LLC
Chambersburg PA
CBHW021145130626
46554CB00005B/1674